Design and Launch an Online

Web Design
Business

in a WEEK

Design and Launch an Online

Web Design Business

in a WEEK

◆ *Tips from Industry Insiders*
◆ *Latest Technology Solutions*
◆ *Hundreds of Tools and Resources*

Entrepreneur Press & Jason R. Rich

EP
Entrepreneur.
Press

Jere L. Calmes, Publisher
Cover Design: Desktop Miracles
Production and Composition: Eliot House Productions

This publication is designed to provide accurate and authoritative information in regard to the subject matter covered. It is sold with the understanding that the publisher is not engaged in rendering legal, accounting or other professional services. If legal advice or other expert assistance is required, the services of a competent professional person should be sought.

Computer icon ©Skocko
Hand icon ©newyear2008

Library of Congress Cataloging-in-Publication Data

Rich, Jason.
  Click start: design and launch an online web design business in a week/by Jason R. Rich.
      p.   cm.
    ISBN-13: 978-1-59918-265-0 (alk. paper)
    ISBN-10: 1-59918-265-3 (alk. paper)
        1. Web site development industry—Management. 2. New business enterprises—Management. I. Title. II. Title: Design and launch an online web design business in a week.
    HD9696.82.A2R53 2009
    006.7'60681--dc22   2008056065

Printed in Canada

13 12 11 10 09   10 9 8 7 6 5 4 3 2 1

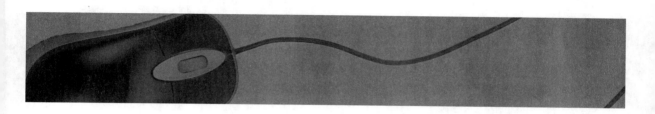

Contents

Chapter 1

The Education and Skills Needed to Be Successful _ _ _ _ 1

Chapter 2

Defining Yourself: Pinpointing Your Skills and Focusing on a Market _____ 17

Chapter 3

Putting Together Your Professional Toolbox _____ 37

Chapter 4

Setting Up Your Business Infrastructure _____ 47

Chapter 5

Online Income Opportunities _____ 79

Chapter 6

Online in One Week or Less _____ 99

Chapter 7

Website Design Fundamentals _____ 129

Chapter 8

Online Payment Options _____ 141

Chapter 9

Creating an Online Portfolio _____ 153

Chapter 10

Marketing Yourself and Your Business in Cyberspace _____ 167

Chapter 11

Marketing Yourself and Your Business in the Real World ____ 191

Chapter 12

Interacting With and Managing Clients _____ 205

Chapter 13

Building Your Online Business _____ 221

Chapter 14

Freelance Experts Speak Out_____ 229

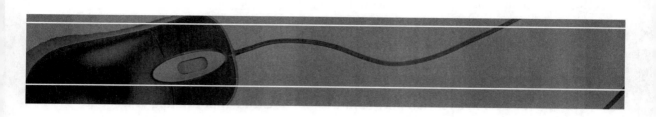

Acknowledgments

*T*hanks to Jere Calmes, Courtney Thurman, and Ronald Young at Entrepreneur Press for inviting me to work on this project. This book is also possible because of the fine editing and design work of Karen Billipp and everyone at Eliot House Productions.

My never-ending love and gratitude goes out to my lifelong friends—Mark, Ellen (as well as Ellen's family), and Ferras

(FerrasMusic.com)—who are all extremely important people in my life—as well as to my other close friends: Kiel James Patrick, Garrick Procter, Christopher Henry, and Chris Coates.

I'd also like to thank my family for all of their support and give a shout-out to my Yorkshire terrier "Rusty" (MyPalRusty.com). Yes, he has his own website, so please check it out! To visit my website, point your web browser to JasonRich.com.

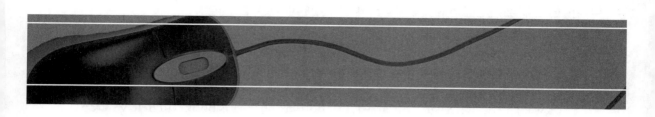

Preface

*A*re you a website designer, graphic artist, or photographer who has spent years learning and fine-tuning your skills and then working as an employee for a company or agency? Do you feel like you're overworked, underpaid, and not being given the opportunity to truly tap into your creativity on the job? Do you find working for someone else unfulfilling?

Perhaps you've already gotten sick of working for someone else. You've quit your full-time job and begun working as an independent freelancer, but you've discovered that finding and landing new clients in your local area is more challenging than you originally anticipated.

Well, if you've decided to utilize your skills, knowledge, and experience as a website designer, graphic artist, or photographer, this book will help you tap the power of the internet for a variety of purposes:

→ To promote and market yourself and your freelance services to a potentially worldwide audience in a cost-effective way

→ To generate new revenue streams by creating an e-commerce website for selling products or downloadables online

→ To develop and implement a business model that allows you to provide your services to clients online, as opposed to in-person

→ To develop an online presence you can use as an online portfolio to showcase your work and impress potential clients

→ To find new potential customers/clients using one of the online services dedicated to matching up freelancers with businesses looking to hire them (such as Guru.com or eLance.com)

As a freelancer, you face many challenges. This book will help you use the internet and create an online presence quickly (within a week or so) and cost effectively. You'll also learn how to better manage your online-based and/or freelance business and handle all of the responsibilities necessary to make it successful—from bookkeeping and record-keeping, to marketing and top-notch customer relations.

What you'll learn from this book is how to position yourself as a skilled and experienced expert in your field, how to identify and market to a target audience, how to use the internet in many different ways to generate revenues as a freelancer (and/or online business operator), how to create an awesome online portfolio to showcase your work, and how to properly manage the online component(s) of your business as a freelance website designer, graphic artist, or photographer.

What you won't learn from this book is the knowledge and skills you need to become a skilled website designer, graphic artist, or photographer. This books begins with the assumption you already have the core education, training, and skills you need to work in one or more of these fields and you've already become proficient doing the type of work a company would hire you to do on a freelance basis, based on your specialty and talents.

As the title of this book suggests, you'll learn how to tap your creative skills, use the various tools available to you, and create an online presence for yourself and your freelance business that will be professional and functional, and will allow you to increase your income. Best of all, you'll learn how to begin using the internet in a variety of different ways and start implementing the strategies described within this book within just one week.

Each chapter of this book guides you through one aspect of taking your freelance business online. In the very last chapter, you'll learn from independent freelancers who have achieved success operating an online presence to boost their respective incomes as website designers, graphic artists, or photographers. From these in-depth interviews, you'll obtain valuable advice on how to be successful as a freelancer conducting business on the web, plus learn how to avoid all-to-common mistakes that can lead to frustration, revenue loss, or total failure.

It's important to understand from the beginning that working in the website design, graphic arts, or photography fields, especially as a freelancer, is extremely competitive. It's true the web gives you access to a much larger pool of potential clients, but it also puts you up against fierce competition. Thus, your ability to generate business and land clients will be based in large part on the quality and impressiveness of your online portfolio and your ability to showcase extremely professional and top-quality work that sets you apart from your competition.

Assuming you can offer truly outstanding work, based on your skills, knowledge, experience, creativity, and talent, you won't necessarily have to compete for new business based on price. Potential clients are often willing to pay a premium for truly superior and specialized work combined with top-notch customer service. If, however, your talent as a website designer, graphic artist, or photographer is just average or below average, you'll find it very difficult to land new clients (whether or not you use the internet), and you'll wind up having to compete solely on price, meaning you'll need to underbid your competition to get work, which dramatically reduces your income potential.

CLICK TIP

Throughout this book, numerous references will be made to your (potential) customers and clients. "Customers" refer to people who will be visiting your e-commerce website and making purchases of products or download-ables. If you're a freelancer who will be soliciting work as a website designer, graphic artist, or photographer using the web, those whom you'll be doing business with are referred to as "clients."

So, if you don't believe your skills and talents are up to par, seriously consider taking steps to fine-tune your talents and build up your portfolio before starting an online business venture. Once you're ready to begin soliciting business or conducting business on the web, however, this book offers comprehensive, yet easy-to-follow, information to help you get started.

Because there are already established tools and services available to website designers, graphic artists, and photographers to help you get yourself online quickly and inexpensively, you won't need to become a programmer or possess any programming skills to get started. What you will need, however, is a creative vision to help you harness your skills, talents, experience, and capabilities in a way that appeals to potential clients and helps to set you apart from your competition.

Now if you're ready to get started exploring all of the different ways you, as a website designer, graphic artist, or photographer, can utilize the internet to establish and grow your freelancing business, it's time to take a closer look at the core education and skills you'll need to truly be successful.

Chapter 1

The Education and Skills Needed to Be Successful

*I*n early 2008, there were more than 156 million websites in existence. While some of these would be considered personal web pages created by amateurs, many are operated by businesses and are used as a sales or promotional tool and to conduct business online. These websites are typically created and maintained by professional website designers, programmers, graphic artists, photographers, and writers who have specialized skills and experience.

The internet has changed the way many companies conduct business. Cyberspace allows even the smallest of business operators to do business with internet-savvy customers throughout the world. By 2010, more than 1.8 billion people worldwide are expected to be web surfers, according to the *Computer Industry Almanac*. That statistic means that the demand for quality websites will continue to grow.

As internet-related technology quickly evolves, the complexity and interactivity of web content has increased dramatically. Today, a website is expected to be easy to navigate, look extremely professional, provide an interactive experience, and incorporate text, graphics, animations, audio, video, and other multimedia content. Websites must also have a defined purpose and provide specific functionality.

These days creating and maintaining a quality website—especially one used for any type of business purposes—require a variety of different skills and areas of expertise. Talented website designers, along with graphic designers, photographers, writers, and programmers who are capable of creating quality online content are in great demand by companies and organizations throughout the world.

For talented and skilled website designers, graphic artists, and photographers, for example, there are many potential career opportunities available.

CLICK TIP

This book will ultimately help you showcase, market, and sell your services and related products as a website designer, graphic designer, or photographer via the web. However, for many freelance professionals, this is only one method of generating business and ongoing revenue. While the web offers you the potential to work with clients and customers from around the world, don't overlook the opportunities available for marketing your products and services locally using more traditional, sometimes called "real-world," methods. Remember that as a freelancer no other marketing or advertising medium is more powerful and more effective than the word-of-mouth advertising generated by your happy customers and clients.

You could land a job working for an established website design or **graphic** arts firm, you could work in-house for a company that has an online presence, or you could work as an independent freelancer and be self-employed.

Click Start: Design and Launch an Online Web Design Business in a Week is written for people who already have the education and skills needed to be a top-notch professional website designer, graphic artist, or photographer and who have opted to be self-employed and work as a freelancer. More specifically, this book is designed to help freelance professionals launch their own online-based business to provide website design and related products and services to customers.

As you're about to discover, whatever your expertise, there are numerous ways to use your skills as a freelance professional to earn an extremely respectable income servicing clients and customers via the web. But while this book will help you create, launch, and maintain an online business as a web professional, it's based on the premise that you already possess the necessary talent, skills, knowledge, and experience to be proficient at your work. In fact, the need to have the right combination of *talent, skills, knowledge, creativity*, and *experience* has been alluded to multiple times. Now you need to look at each of these prerequisites more closely so you understand what is required for you to truly be successful. You'll quickly discover that unless you possess all of these traits, you'll be at a tremendous disadvantage.

Natural Talent

Talent refers to your ability to take the specialized knowledge and formal training you acquire and put it to practical use in real-world situations. As you'll quickly discover, becoming a successful website designer, graphic artist, or photographer requires a unique set of specialized skills that can be learned. However, this is only one piece of the formula.

To be successful in any or all of these fields, you must also possess a natural talent and flair for your work. You must have an incredible amount of creativity and artistic ability, traits that cannot be taught. Being able to seamlessly combine creativity and artistic ability with your learned skills is essential.

For example, some website designers utilize specialized software, like Adobe Dreamweaver CS3 (CS4), to program and design websites. People can take classes or teach themselves to be extremely proficient using this software. They can learn how to utilize every command and feature offered by the software, and how to effectively use Dreamweaver in conjunction with a variety of other website design and graphics creation tools. However, if these same people don't have the natural creativity and artistic ability to create professional looking, highly functional, visually appealing websites that achieve their intended objectives, their work probably won't meet the needs of their clients.

Natural talent is all about creativity, artistic ability, personal taste, and the ability to tap into skills not taught in traditional classes in order to excel. Good website designers, for example, must have an instinct for what looks good visually and be able to use their creativity to provide a truly unique and rich experience for the visitors to the websites they're creating.

Skills

Skills refer to acquired expertise using tools of your trade. If you're a website designer, it might mean being an expert HTML programmer and having proficiency with Dreamweaver and a variety of other website design tools.

CLICK TIP

Creativity refers to your natural ability to use your imagination and think outside of the box as you approach your various freelance projects and work with your clients.

Skills can be acquired by completing a degree or certification program, taking individual classes, reading books, participating in online training programs, or a variety of other methods. Based on the career path you choose to pursue, acquiring and constantly working to enhance your core skill set will be essential to your success as a freelancer. Few fields are as rapidly changing as the professions related to the web.

Knowledge

For the purposes of this book, *knowledge* refers to all of the information you possess that allows you to meet the needs of your clients. It also refers to the knowledge you possess about finding and landing new clients, and operating your own business as a self-employed freelancer: your ability to work well with your clients, including your customer service skills, manage your personal and company finances (bookkeeping skills), and handle the day-to-day responsibilities of operating your online-based business. Your knowledge also takes into account the skills you possess and the know-how you have that allows you to fully use your natural talents and creativity.

The knowledge you'll need to successfully work as a freelance web professional goes beyond the core skills needed to design and create websites, logos, illustrations, or photographs. Chapter 4, for example, will help you acquire the knowledge you need to set up your business's infrastructure, while Chapter 6 will assist you in putting all of your knowledge to work as you get the online aspect of your business up and running. From Chapter 8, you'll acquire the knowledge you need about online payment options, and from Chapters 9 and 10 you'll discover information you need to effectively promote and market the online part of your business.

Experience

As you put all of your natural talent, skills, and knowledge together and begin successfully working with customers and clients, you'll develop real world experience as well as a portfolio of work that you can showcase to future clients and customers. In these fields you are more apt to get hired based on the quality of your past work and less apt to be hired based on the skills listed on your resume. Nobody cares that you've become proficient using Dreamweaver, for example. What potential clients care about is that you have the skills and natural talent needed to create a website that perfectly meets their needs and wants.

Your ability to create a professional portfolio of your work that truly showcases your abilities and sets you apart from your competition is your most important tool for generating business and achieving credibility among prospective clients and customers. Chapter 9 focuses on creating an impressive portfolio, one that adequately showcases your skills, knowledge, and natural abilities, while at the same time proves you have what it takes to exceed the wants, needs, and expectations of your clients.

Formal Training Is Not Required, but It Certainly Helps

One of the most alluring aspects of working as a freelance website designer, graphic artist, or photographer with an online-based business model is that while it's essential that you possess the right combination of talents, skills, knowledge, and experience, you don't necessarily need a college or graduate degree to be successful. Many colleges and universities do offer well-established degree or certificate programs for these fields, but a degree is not required to be successful. Likewise, you don't need any special licenses.

CLICK TIP

Before you can launch an online business and begin offering your services, consider developing a specialty or area of expertise, and then determining the best target market for the services/products you'll be offering.

Obviously, the more specialized education you have in your field, the bigger your advantage. However, most companies hire website designers, programmers, graphic artists, and photographers based on their proven skills and experience, not on their educational background.

Top-quality websites and other print or online content can often be created by people who possess different skills, knowledge, and professional backgrounds. The next few sections of this chapter focus on career paths you could follow in order to develop the skills and knowledge you'll need to launch your online website business.

Website Designer

The job title web designer can mean a lot of different things. Companies requiring the services of a web designer often have a very broad definition of what the job entails. A tremendous variation exists in the skills and knowledge required to successfully perform the work.

As the job title suggests, a website designer designs, creates (programs), and/or maintains websites. Doing this might require extensive HTML programming knowledge as well as proficiency creating code using other popular programming languages, such as CSS and JavaScript, layout and design skills, graphic design skills, database management skills, and the ability to manage the sites once they're operational. In some cases, website designers create just the look and layout of a website, which is then actually created (programmed) by one or more programmers. In other cases, they just maintain the site.

Job titles like website designer, webmaster, web developer, and web producer are used somewhat interchangeably. However, some companies differentiate among these job titles by related responsibilities. For example, a web master might be hired to maintain a website designed by a website designer and programmed by a web developer (programmer).

A website designer who is responsible for the overall layout, design, and organization of a website, and for establishing its functionality and purpose, will often have some graphic arts training and background because much of this work involves creativity and artistic skill. A web producer who is often responsible for creating the content to be incorporated into a website might have a journalism, writing, graphic arts, or marketing/PR background.

In general, web designers create the pages, layout, animations, and graphics for a website. These people are typically responsible for the "front end" of a website and create the look and feel of a site (its interface), while web developers/programmers handle the "back end" of a site.

As a website designer (or someone involved with creating and maintaining websites), it's essential that you stay abreast of the latest technologies, trends, and applications being used in the field, which means constantly fine-tuning and updating your skills and your ability to use specific programs and development tools. For example, just a few years ago being proficient using Microsoft FrontPage was absolutely essential. Today, however, this tool,

---

CLICK TIP

As a website designer, there are a wide range of services and products you can offer through an online business based on your area of expertise. Chapter 5 will help you develop multiple potential revenue streams given the products and/or services you opt to offer.

which was once an industry standard, is considered outdated. Instead, programs like Adobe's Dreamweaver, Flash, PhotoShop, and Illustrator are the tools typically used to create and maintain websites.

Not only must website designers be proficient using all of the latest tools, they must also have top-notch communication skills to be able to interact well with clients, have the ability to define and understand client needs, and then be able to develop a website that properly addresses those needs.

Education and Skills Needed

Most companies that hire in-house website designers look for someone with at least a bachelor's degree in graphic design, visual arts, fine arts, or in a related field. Many schools even offer specific degrees in website design.

If you don't have the wherewithal to pursue a four-year degree, there are two-year (or shorter) certification programs offered by accredited colleges and universities that can equip you with the knowledge and skills to land a job in this field. For example, some schools offer a Certified Internet Webmaster (CIW) course.

The core knowledge and skills needed to pursue web design can also be self-taught, acquired from watching training videos or by reading how-to books. These skills can also be acquired by attending seminars or adult education programs. Self-paced online training courses are also available.

Thus, there is no universally accepted way to prepare for this work, and no internationally recognized set of requirements. As someone who plans to pursue this work as a freelancer operating an online business, what will count most is your portfolio and your ability to showcase your competence and skills in real-world situations.

To learn more about educational opportunities related to becoming a website designer, visit these websites:

- ➡ Adobe eLearning Solutions: adobe.com/resources/elearning
- ➡ ITT Technical Institute: itt-tech.edu
- ➡ Online Web & Graphic Design Programs: classesusa.com/featured schools/programs/featured_web.cap
- ➡ Top 10 Computer Schools: top10computerschools.com

➡ Web Design School Review: webdesignschoolreview.com
➡ Web Design Schools: webdesignschools.com

CLICK TIP

As you'll learn in Chapter 9, regardless of how much formal training you have and what programs or tools you're proficient using,
what will ultimately get you hired is the sampling of your work that you're able to
showcase in a portfolio. Potential customers and clients don't care what you know or
how many certifications, degrees, or courses you've completed. What they care about is
your ability to successfully do the work that's required, within the predetermined time
frame, and at an affordable rate. Ultimately, your portfolio will be your most powerful
tool for landing new business and building up your credibility with potential customers
and clients. A portfolio is a look at your best work, displayed in a way that best showcases it to potential clients or customers. For website designers, for example, this might
include creating your own site that provides links to other sites you've worked on, plus
a sampling of your best work.

Earning Potential

According to the *Occupational Outlook Handbook—2008–2009 Edition*, (U.S.
Department of Labor Statistics), the salary range for a web designer in 2007
was between $47,000 and $71,500, while a web developer earned between
$54,750 and $81,500. A senior web developer earned between $71,000 and
$102,000, and a web administrator earned between $49,750 and $74,750.

Working as a freelancer, you have the opportunity to set your own schedule and rates. Thus, assuming you have the skills and ability to land clients,
your earning potential will be tied directly to how hard you work and the work
schedule you keep. Remember, as you establish yourself as a freelancer, it'll
take time to develop a base of customers and begin earning a steady paycheck.
Also, you'll find yourself tied closely to your work. After all, if you're not on
the job as a freelancer, you're not earning money. Unlike working for an
employer, there are no paid vacations.

Website Programmer

If you plan to pursue a career as a freelance web programmer, your primary responsibilities will be to handle the back-end of a website. Thus, creativity and artistic abilities are far less important than your ability to generate program code using one or more programming languages and/or website development tools.

As a programmer, you will transform the design concepts created by a website designer or graphic artist, for example, into a fully functional website using your programming skills. You will also use text, graphic, and multimedia content created by others. It's the programmer's job to create, test, and maintain the programming behind a website. As a result, programmers spend the majority of their time working at a computer.

Education and Skills Needed

According to the *Occupational Outlook Handbook—2008–2009 Edition*, in 2006 eight out of ten computer programmers held an associate's degree or higher; nearly half held a bachelor's degree; and two out of ten held a graduate degree. Again, if you'll be working as a freelancer, your formal education will be less important than your ability to showcase your proficiency handling the programming work you're soliciting from potential clients.

Earning Potential

In 2007 the starting salary for computer programmers averaged $49,928, according to the National Association of Colleges and Employers. The Bureau of Labor Statistics adds, "almost eight out of ten computer programmers held an associate's degree or higher in 2006; nearly half held a bachelor's degree, and two out of ten held a graduate degree. Job prospects will be best for applicants with a bachelor's degree and experience with a variety of programming languages and tools."

Graphic Artist

A graphic artist or graphic designer is someone who uses graphics and artwork to communicate information in print and online. This can include everything from creating company logos to designing letterheads, product packaging, advertising visuals, and artwork for websites. Working as a graphic artist requires a tremendous amount of creativity and natural artistic ability combined with proficiency using various art tools, including popular graphics software packages.

Many colleges and universities offer a bachelor's degree in graphic design. If you'll be designing graphics for websites or web pages themselves, you'll want to focus your education on computerized design and pursue courses in advertising, marketing, and website design.

In addition to traditional colleges and universities, associate degrees and certificates in graphic design can be earned from two- and three-year professional schools. According to the National Association of Schools of Art and Design, there are more than 250 postsecondary institutions currently offering programs in art and design.

In 2006, approximate 261,000 people held jobs as graphic artists, and about 25 percent of them were self-employed. Between 2006 and 2016, employment for graphic designers is expected to grow by 10 percent. The *Occupational Outlook Handbook* reports, "Graphic designers with website design and animation experience will especially be needed as demand increases for design projects or interactive media—websites, video games, cellular telephones, personal digital assistants, and other technology. Demand for graphic designers will also increase as advertising firms create print and web marketing and promotional materials for a growing number of products and services."

Education and Skills Needed

Regardless of the education you pursue, a graphic artist/designer must be highly creative and have superior communications and problem-solving skills. Natural artistic ability, a keen eye for detail, and the ability to showcase your work using a portfolio will prove far more important when soliciting new clients than describing your formal education, especially if you're working as a freelancer. Research shows that graphic designers with a broad liberal arts education and experience in marketing and business management are best prepared to meet the demands of their clients when developing communications strategies.

To learn more about educational opportunities related to graphic arts, visit these websites:

➡ American Institute of Graphic Arts: aiga.org
➡ Art Schools Directory: artschools.com or allartschools.com
➡ Graphic Arts School Directory: graphicartsschools.com
➡ National Association of Schools of Art and Design: nasad.arts-ac credit.org
➡ School of Visual Arts: schoolofvisualarts.edu
➡ The Art Institutes: education.org/artinstitutes/aiDesignHome.php

Earning Potential

As of May 2006, the median salary for graphic designers was between $30,900 and $53,310 per year. In 2007 the American Institute of Graphic Arts (aiga.org) reported that the average salary for an entry-level graphic artist was $35,000, while senior graphic designers earned upwards of $62,000 per year. Solo designers who worked on a freelance basis or under contract to another company earned an average annual salary of $60,000 in 2007.

Photographer

A photographer is someone who takes photographs. There are commercial photographers, wedding photographers, nature photographers, news photographers (photojournalists), portrait photographers, fine art photographers, and countless other specialties. A good photographer is able to tell a story

---

CLICK TIP

Working as a photographer requires a significant investment in photographic equipment, including one or more cameras plus lenses, accessories, lighting, studio equipment, etc. (based on your needs and specialty). Today's photographers must also be skilled using photo editing and archiving software, such as Photoshop CS3 (CS4).

---

with a single image. In addition to having an eye for photography, a tremendous amount of creativity and technical know-how are beneficial. In 2006, the U.S. Department of Labor Statistics reported that 122,000 people held a job as a photographer in America, and that more than half of those people were self-employed (freelancers).

The ability to use a digital and/or traditional film camera, various lenses, and potentially lighting and/or studio equipment to capture images is essential. Today's photographer also needs to be computer savvy and proficient using photo editing and archiving software, such as PhotoShop CS3 (CS4).

A typical freelance photographer has one or two specialties. For such photographers, a web-based business can be used in several ways:

➡ As an interactive, online portfolio to showcase your work and solicit new clients
➡ As a way to showcase and sell photographs and related products
➡ As a way to interact with existing clients and customers

Education and Skills Needed

The skills and knowledge needed to be a professional photographer can be self-taught. It's possible to obtain the knowledge through working as an intern or apprentice for another photographer. There are also many photography vocational schools that offer certifications in photography, and some accredited colleges and universities offer degree programs.

While anyone can learn how to operate a camera, it's much harder to develop or be taught the artistic skills, hand-eye coordination, and creativity needed to be a top-notch photographer. To learn more about careers in photography, contact one of these organizations:

➡ American Society of Media Photographers: asmp.org
➡ Brooks Institute: brooks.edu
➡ National Press Photographers Association: nppa.org
➡ New York Institute of Photography: nyip.com
➡ Photography Schools Directories: photographyschools.com or art-photo graphy-schools.com
➡ Photoshop World: photoshopworld.com

➡ Professional Photographers of America: ppa.com

Earning Potential

The salaries earned by photographers working freelance can vary greatly, based on a variety of factors, including their specialty. In 2006, the *Occupational Outlook Handbook* reported that the salary range for a photographer was between $15,540 and $56,640.

How and Where to Obtain the Education and Skills You Require

Demand for your work as a freelancer will be based mainly on your proven abilities, your portfolio, and your ability to solicit customers. Thus, learning how to market and promote yourself online and in the real world will prove to be an essential skill.

When it comes to acquiring the skills and knowledge needed to pursue work as a website designer, graphic artist, or photographer, you have five primary options:

1. Pursue a four-year degree from an accredited college or university.
2. Pursue an associate's degree or certificate from a professional or vocational school, or accredited distance-learning program.
3. Participate in classes, seminars, and workshops offered through various professional organizations, adult education programs, and community colleges.
4. Teach yourself the required skills by reading how-to books, and watching training videos.
5. Participate in an internship/apprenticeship program (paid or unpaid) with another photographer or a photography studio.

In these fields, gaining real-world experience before starting out as a self-employed freelancer is extremely beneficial, especially if you're self-taught and have not pursued a formal education in your selected field. The time and financial commitment required to pursue any of these career paths will vary greatly depending on the option(s) you choose.

Always Keep Learning

Regardless of what career path you ultimately follow, understand that the learning process is never-endinge. To be successful, you need to work continuously to enhance and perfect your professional skills and knowledge. At the same time, because you're contemplating operating an online business, you need to invest the time and resources necessary to create and maintain your online presence and to learn the core business skills required of the self-employed.

Even if you're exceptionally talented and have the natural artistic abilities and creativity that allows you to set yourself apart and excel as a freelance website professional, you will face intense competition. While the internet can be used as a powerful business tool to help you find and land customers, you'll be completing head on for business with the thousands of other freelancers and established firms based in the United States and overseas.

As you'll discover, there are always freelancers willing to work harder, provide more services, charge less money, and offer faster turn-around times, and who are more talented than you. In Chapter 2, however, you'll discover how you can benefit and give yourself an edge by carefully defining your area of expertise. Your ability to create and showcase your talent and skills of a portfolio will also be essential, as will your ability to set yourself apart from your competition by doing a better job marketing yourself and your online business (topics covered in Chapters 9, 10, and 11).

Another key to your long-term success as a freelance website designer, graphic artist, or photographer conducting business on the web is your ability to offer top-notch customer service (covered in Chapter 12). Not only is customer service essential for building loyalty and repeat business, it also helps you generate positive word-of-mouth advertising, one of the most powerful ways you can generate new business.

Creativity and Artistic Ability Are Essential

Unfortunately, the two key ingredients needed to be a successful web professional—creativity and artistic ability—are not skills that can easily be taught in school or acquired by reading books or participating in a training program.

People are either born with these natural abilities, or they're not. Those that are have a definite advantage in these fields, especially if the natural abilities are cultivated, fine-tuned, reinforced, and improved upon over time with additional training, practice, and guidance.

If you give two freelance website designers identical assignments, the end result will probably be vastly different. Likewise, if you give two people a camera and tell them to photograph a specific event or object, their photographs will be different, despite the fact that the subject matter is identical.

Artistic people learn to incorporate their creativity and natural abilities into their work, which is what sets them apart from their competition, even if they otherwise have the same formal training and identical tools. The ability to harness your creativity and use it to your utmost advantage, while always striving to meet the demands of your clients, is crucial to your long-term success, especially if you're conducting some or all of your business via the web.

Finding Your Own Niche

By now, you should understand that website design, graphic arts, and photography are extremely diverse fields. Pursuing one or more requires specialized knowledge and education, as well as natural artistic ability and creativity. As you establish yourself as a professional freelancer working in any of these fields, you'll want and need to develop an area of expertise or specialty—for a variety of reasons. For example, having a specialty and being considered an expert in your field allows you to charge top dollar for your services, and it is easier to seek out and land new clients/customers in need of the services you offer.

The next chapter focuses on defining yourself as a freelance professional and should help you pinpoint your unique skill set and area of expertise. At the same time, it teaches you how to focus on a special market or customer base in order to generate business. These strategies are useful when planning and operating the online component of your business.

Chapter 2

Defining Yourself: Pinpointing Your Skills and Focusing on a Market

*N*o matter what products or services you'll be offering as a freelance website designer, graphic artist, or photographer, you'll face a tremendous amount of competition, not just from fellow freelancers based in the United States but also from people overseas who are also using the internet to reach potential new clients and customers. Because you're working in an industry that's primarily based on creativity and one's ability to fully utilize various tools and resources, what will ultimately help you land new business is your ability to offer customers/clients what they want, when they want it, and at a competitive price. In addition to offering products and services that are equivalent or superior to those your competition offers, you must be able to effectively market to those you perceive to be your target market to be successful.

This chapter focuses on the talents that will help you achieve success with your online business venture. They are:

1. Your ability to define and differentiate yourself and the products and/or services you plan to offer.
2. Your ability to pinpoint and effectively showcase your skills, experience, knowledge, creativity, and potential to customers/clients interested specifically in what you have to offer.
3. Your ability to focus on marketing your products/services to one or more specific target audiences in order to use the time, money, and effort you invest in marketing and promoting your business.

As you learned from Chapter 1, having the proper credentials—natural talent, skills, knowledge, experience, and training—to be a successful website designer, graphic artist, or photographer is certainly important. The next step involves focusing on what you have to offer and creating a specialty or niche for yourself that sets you apart from the competition and helps you create a demand for your products and services.

If you opt to pursue work as a freelance website designer, for example, you might choose to specialize in developing e-commerce websites or websites for musicians and music groups. Or you could specialize in developing websites for other specific purposes or for a narrowly defined type of customer or client working in a specific field or industry. This work might involve doing customized work for clients or creating website templates that you can sell online as a downloadable product.

As a graphic designer, you might opt to specialize in creating company logos or to establish yourself as an expert at creating commercial illustrations, product packaging, or advertising. A photographer might focus on wedding photography, commercial photography, freelance photojournalism, or creating products such as greeting cards, mouse pads, T-shirts, and posters and then sell directly to consumers online.

CLICK TIP

The easiest and best way to generate business and find new clients is to establish yourself as an expert in your field and to develop a reputation for being a specialist in that area. Then, you can showcase your work to a targeted audience and use positive word-of-mouth advertising. Referrals from your past and existing clients/customers will ultimately become one of your most powerful and effective marketing tools.

Fine-Tuning Your Skill Set

Once you decided how you want to harness your interests, skills, knowledge, experience, and natural abilities in order to earn a living as a freelancer, it is absolutely necessary to stay up-to-date on all of the latest trends, tools, and technologies being used in your field. Thus, after determining the areas you want to specialize in, you'll need to become proficient using all of the resources at your disposal to identify and fulfill the wants and needs of your clients. Furthermore, because you've decided to do the majority of your work using the internet as your primary marketing and communications tool, you need to ensure that your online presence properly showcases your offerings to the right audience.

Because technology and trends change so quickly, it is your ongoing responsibility and challenge to keep your skills and knowledge current, and that you're able to meet the wants and needs of your customers/clients. In addition to reading trade publications relevant to your line of work as well as the industries your clients work in, you'll want to pursue new training opportunities and make it a goal to continuously expand and fine-tune your skill set.

Developing a Specialty

The titles website designer, graphic artist, and photographer encompass many specialties. While you could promote yourself as a jack of all trades in hopes of generating the most interest possible from the broadest base of potential clients/customers, taking this approach will result in your having to complete head-on with even more competition. In fact, it'll be all too easy for you to get lost in the crowd, making it hard for potential clients/customers to find you. Thus, the choice to hire you or purchase what you're offering will become that much more difficult.

Simply by differentiating yourself by developing a specialty, you can more easily promote what it is you're offering to a more narrowly defined audience. This will help to set yourself apart from your competition, promote yourself as a true expert in your field, and allow you to potentially charge a premium for your products/services.

As a freelance website designer, you'll face competition from other free-lancers and website development firms willing to offer their services to anyone, an individual or a company, at absolutely rock bottom prices. If, however, you specialize in a particular type of website design or focus on creating websites for a specific industry or specialty, you can charge a premium for your proven expertise and unique, specialized knowledge.

For example, online business operators who wish to create an e-commerce website from scratch have a unique set of needs and require websites with very specific functionality. Given the growth of the internet, there are many new businesses launching every day. Catering your website design business to

---

CLICK TIP

If you'll be selling products or downloadables online, you'll want to differentiate these from the competition and truly understand your target market. Doing so will help you be able to charge premium prices for your offerings. Plus, you'll be able to find and market to the people or companies most likely to want or need what you're offering.

startup e-commerce operators, for example, and being able to showcase experience and expertise in this field will help you to set yourself apart from other website designers. Use the questionnaire in Figure 2.1 to help you clearly define the objectives for your business.

Figure 2.1: **YOUR BUSINESS OBJECTIVE QUESTIONNAIRE**

The following worksheet will help you summarize your goals and credentials, and develop an initial direction for your business. Answer these questions as thoroughly as possible.

- What primary product(s) or service(s) do you plan to offer online? Why?

- What is your goal for launching an online presence for your business?

- If you're offering any type of service, what additional skills or experience do you need to be effective working with clients online, as opposed to in person?

- What will set you apart from your competition?

- Who will be your primary target market?

- Who will be your secondary target market?

- How will you price your products/services?

- What specifically will you do to add value to your products/services, beyond what your competition is doing?

- What credentials do you possess that will help you stand out from your competition and appeal to your potential customers/clients?

- Within the next few months, what skills, knowledge, or education will you acquire to ensure you'll be qualified to offer the most cutting-edge products/services, based on customer demand and current trends in your field?

- How you will position yourself as a specialist or expert in your field? What will you do to promote your reputation and build confidence among current and potential customers/clients?

- What do you anticipate will be the top five objections, misconceptions, or obstacles you'll need to overcome before a potential customer/client becomes a paying customer/client? How will you overcome these challenges?

> ## CLICK TIP
>
> As you launch your new online business, consider focusing initially on just one specialty product or service. Later, you can grow your business by offering additional products/services and by expanding your target market. Again, do everything you can to establish yourself as an expert or specialist in your field. Focus on catering to the specific needs of a niche customer base in order to help set yourself apart from your competition.

Getting to Know Your Niche Markets

Once you have a business objective and determined how you intend to make money through your online business, the next major step involves pinpointing and then focusing in on your target market. This is a three-step process:

1. Understanding who comprises your target market
2. Effectively reaching your target market, both with your website and your advertising, marketing, public relations, and promotions
3. Properly catering to your target market's wants and needs

This section helps you define your target audience, pinpoints the audience your website will cater to, and helps you decide how you'll best reach that market. Remember, it's to your benefit to know and understand as much about your target customer as possible. This typically requires that you conduct research.

Ultimately, as you begin to develop your website's content and all of your marketing materials, you'll want to put yourself in your target customers' shoes and think the way they think. If you're a middle-aged male targeting young, single females with your products/services, this imagining might pose more of a challenge than catering to an audience you readily relate to and share many common interests.

Establish Your Niche

Most startup online businesspeople find it infinitely easier to select products to sell and/or services to offer that cater to a small niche market. By doing this, it becomes easier to understand the potential customer base, address its wants, needs, and concerns, and specifically focus your website's content, and marketing materials, on this narrowly-defined audience.

A niche market can be any group of people that you define to be your target audience. It can be based on a single defining factor, such as a special interest. The more narrowly you define your audience, the easier it is to ascertain its wants and needs, and fous on them. Of course, your product/service might appeal to several unique target audiences, in which case you'd want to define and address each of these audiences separately in order to maximize your customer base and the sales potential for your offerings. It's always a good strategy, however, to begin focusing on what you believe is the biggest and easier target audience to reach and then broaden your efforts from there as your business becomes more established.

Before you can define your niche market, spend as much time as is necessary to get to know absolutely everything there is to know about the product(s)/service(s) you'll be selling. Also, invest the time needed to learn about competing products/services so you can explain exactly why what you're offering is superior, more useful, more cost-effective, more efficient, and/or packed with more features. Ultimately, you want to become an expert in your field. By the time you start selling your product/service(s), you should be able to answer absolutely any question about it.

CLICK TIP

As you do your product research, keep a written list of the most common questions people have or may have about your products and services. You want to address these questions on your website and in your marketing materials. Creating and posting a FAQ (frequently asked questions) document on your site is beneficial. It can save you a lot of time by not having to answer e-mails and phone calls from individual customers.

Defining Your Audience

You already know how important it is to understand and know your target audience. Use the worksheet in Figure 2.2 to help you fine-tune exactly who comprises this customer base. Think about what your product/service is, who it primarily appeals to, who is purchasing it, who is using it, what needs it addresses, how it potentially solves a problem, and who benefits the most from using it. The worksheets in Figures 2.3 and 2.4 should help to further refine these issues.

Figure 2.2: **TARGET AUDIENCE WORKSHEET**

Directions: For each category, check all that apply to your primary target audience. Once you've carefully narrowed down your target audience, complete this worksheet a second time to define your secondary audience for your product. The relevance of some of these questions will vary depending on whether your target customer/client is a business or an individual consumer.

Target Company Type (if applicable): _____

Industry: _____

Company Size: _____ **Number of Employees:** _____

Business Focus: _____

Gender: ❑ Male ❑ Female ❑ Not applicable

Marital Status: ❑ Single ❑ Married ❑ Divorced
❑ Widowed ❑ Not applicable

Age: ❑ Child ❑ Teenager ❑ Age 18 to 24
❑ Age 25 to 49 ❑ Age 50 to 65 ❑ Age 66+
❑ Not applicable

Race: ❑ White ❑ African American ❑ Hispanic
❑ Asian ❑ Other:_____ ❑ Not applicable

Sexual Orientation: ❑ Straight ❑ Gay ❑ Bisexual ❑ Not applicable

Income Level: ❑ Under $15,000 per year
❑ $15,001 to $25,000 per year
❑ $25,001 to $45,000 per year
❑ $45,001 to $55,000 per year
❑ $55,001 to $99,999 per year

Figure 2.2: **TARGET AUDIENCE WORKSHEET,** continued

Income Level:
- ❏ $100,000 to $500,000 per year
- ❏ $500,000 to $999,999 per year
- ❏ $1,000,000 to $5,000,000 per year
- ❏ $5,000,001+ per year
- ❏ Not applicable

Education Level:
- ❏ Some high school
- ❏ High school graduate
- ❏ College graduate
- ❏ Advanced degree
- ❏ Not applicable

Occupation: _____   ❏ Not applicable

Religion: _____   ❏ Not applicable

Geographic Region:

Specific City/State—Specify: _____
- ❏ United States
- ❏ Canada
- ❏ Europe
- ❏ Asia
- ❏ South America
- ❏ North America
- ❏ Africa
- ❏ Australia
- ❏ Antarctica
- ❏ Not applicable

Physical Attributes:
- ❏ Tall
- ❏ Short
- ❏ Average height

Figure 2.2: **TARGET AUDIENCE WORKSHEET,** continued

Physical	❑ Thin
Attributes:	❑ Overweight
	❑ Average weight
	❑ Not applicable

Housing:
❑ Owns home
❑ Rents home
❑ Rents apartment
❑ Owns condo
❑ Rents condo
❑ Lives with parents
❑ Lives with roommate(s)
❑ Lives with spouse
❑ Lives with spouse and children
❑ Other: _____
❑ Not applicable

Business Owner:
❑ Business that operates from an office
❑ Business that operates from a home office
❑ Business that operates from a factory
❑ Business that operates from a warehouse
❑ Other: _____
❑ Not applicable

Primary
Computer and
Internet Usage:
❑ At home
❑ At work
❑ Internet café/Wi-fi location
❑ Wireless PDA or Smartphone
❑ Not online

Figure 2.2: **TARGET AUDIENCE WORKSHEET,** continued

Hobbies/
Special Interests: _____   ❏ Not applicable

Club/Association
Membership: _____   ❏ Not applicable

Spending/Shopping Habits:
    ❏ Typically shops at retail stores
    ❏ Shops often via mail order
    ❏ Comfortable shopping online
    ❏ Readily uses credit cards
    ❏ Readily uses a debit card
    ❏ Writes checks for purchases
    ❏ Possesses a PayPal account
    ❏ Has below average or no credit
    ❏ Utilizes a line of credit or payment terms with vendors

Driving Habits:
    ❏ Drives a compact vehicle/hatchback
    ❏ Drives an SUV/van
    ❏ Drives a pick-up truck
    ❏ Drives a sports car
    ❏ Drives a luxury sedan
    ❏ Drives a hybrid vehicle
    ❏ Owns vehicle
    ❏ Leases vehicle
    ❏ Drives less than 15,000 miles per year
    ❏ Drives more than 15,000 miles per year
    ❏ Commutes daily to work
    ❏ Carpools
    ❏ Other: _____

Media Habits:
    ❏ Primarily watches TV
    ❏ Primarily reads newspapers

Figure 2.2: **TARGET AUDIENCE WORKSHEET,** continued

Media Habits: ❑ Primarily reads consumer-oriented magazines
❑ Primarily reads industry-oriented magazines
❑ Primarily surfs the web
❑ Not applicable

Other Relevant Attribute: _____

Other Relevant Attribute: _____

Other Relevant Attribute: _____

After defining your primary and secondary audience for your product, answer the questions in Figure 2.3 as they apply to what you'll be selling and to whom you'll be selling. As you answer these questions on a separate sheet of paper, be as specific as possible. Also, don't forget to put yourself in your target customers' shoes and think the way they would think (taking into account their needs, wants, and concerns).

Based on the information you compiled within this worksheet, you should now have a relatively detailed profile of your primary customer base as well as your potential secondary markets. Now, you can proceed by learning as much as possible about the people who make up your target market and begin formulating all of the ways your product will address their wants and needs.

After defining your primary and secondary audience for your service(s), answer the questions in Figure 2.4 as they apply to what you'll be selling and to whom you'll be selling. As you answer these questions on a separate sheet of paper, be as specific as possible. Also, don't forget to put yourself in your target customers' shoes and think the way they would think (taking into account their needs, wants, and concerns).

Figure 2.3: **PRODUCT WORKSHEET**

This worksheet applies only if you'll be selling one or more products online.

- What about your product will appeal to your target audience? (Be sure to list specific features, functions, selling points, etc.)

- How, when, and why will your target customer use the product?

- What needs does your product address?

- How does your product satisfy your target customer's wants?

- Why would someone want to buy your product?

- What problems, challenges, or obstacles can your product help the customer overcome? How will it make lives happier, better, easier, less stressful, more entertaining, etc.?

- What are the biggest and best benefits or features that your product offers?

- Describe why your product is worth the money people will spend for it.

- Why should someone use your product as opposed to a completing product?

- What do you anticipate the biggest objections your target customer will have regarding your product? How can these objections be overcome?

- What misconceptions might your target customer have about your product? What information will you need to convey to help overcome these misconceptions quickly?

- Why should someone purchase the product from your online business?

Figure 2.4: **SERVICE WORKSHEET**

This worksheet applies only if you'll be marketing and/or selling services online.

- What specific services will you be offering?

- How will you offer these services?

- What steps will you take to develop a true understanding of the wants and needs of each of your clients?

- What industry or topic-specific knowledge or experience do you possess that will help you be successful in catering to your clients' needs?

- How will your services differ from your competition?

- What makes you qualified to offer these services?

- How will you showcase your proficiency in being able to expertly offer these services?

- How will you price your services? How will this pricing compare to your competition?

- How will your services help your clients? What problems will you help solve? What solutions will you offer?

- What steps will you take to offer personalized customer service and attention to your customers?

- What will you do to add value to your offerings beyond what your competition offers?

- What are the top three qualities about you and your credentials, reputation and experience that will appeal to your potential clients and make you marketable?

- Why should someone hire you, as opposed to your competition? List at least five "selling points" designed to convince someone to hire you.

- What guarantees can you offer in regard to customer satisfaction and meeting your deadlines?

- If you'll be charging more than your competition, what extras or benefits can your clients expect?

Figure 2.4: **SERVICE WORKSHEET,** continued

- If you'll be charging less than your competition, how will this negatively impact your ability to offer top-notch and personalized service while maintaining a competitive edge as a business operator?

Doing Your Market Research

Approach your market research from several angles. First, focus on the product or service you'll be selling and learn as much as you can about the people it appeals to. Research what your competition is doing to market the same or similar offerings. What approach is your competition taking? Who is their target audience? What primary marketing message is your competition using? Based on your knowledge of the product and your target audience, how can you improve or build on what your competition is doing in order to attract your own customers?

Next, do as much research about your target audience as possible. Based on the profile you create for your primary audience, learn as much as possible about their likes and dislikes, their wants, their needs, and what problems they're facing in their daily lives. Focus on how you can use this knowledge to generate as much interest in your product as possible. How much effort will you have to put into educating your target customer about the products/services you'll be selling? What information will you need to convey? What is the best way to convey this information in a succinct, easy-to-understand, cost-effective way that will capture your target audience's attention?

The internet itself is an extremely powerful market research tool. Also, take a close look at whatever information is available from the manufacturer or distributor(s) of the product you're planning to sell (if applicable) as well as whatever materials and information are available from your competition.

Addressing the Wants and Needs of Your Customers

No matter what you're selling, every consumer buys based on a need or desire. As someone about to begin selling one or more products/services online, it's important to understand that the need your customer has for what you offer can be real or can be perceived. In other words, the consumer might really and truly need the product/service or with the help of your marketing become convinced that it is needed in order to solve a problem, make life somehow easier, or add happiness to life on some level. This latter is a perceived need, and it can be just as powerful as a real need in terms of influencing someone's buying habits. As you begin selling, your goal is to make your audience think "I need this now!" and get them to ask themselves "How did I ever live without it?"

In addition to needs, people have wants and desires. Most people and businesses also have some discretionary income they can use to make purchases that can satisfy various wants and desires. All marketing and advertising is designed to appeal to a customer's wants, needs, or both. If a want or need doesn't actually exist for something you're selling, it becomes your job to create a perceived want or need in the customer's mind. This, however, can be tricky. Executives at advertising agencies, marketing firms, and public relations firms spend years fine-tuning their skills and mastering techniques for influencing peoples' buying habits. Assuming you don't have the budget to hire an advertising agency or public relations firm, these are skills you have to learn yourself.

The approach you take, however, must be customized for the product/service you're selling and for the audience you're targeting. A certain website design, for example, may work extremely well for selling one specific type of product/service to a specific target audience, but it might not work at all for another product/service designed to reach a different audience altogether.

One of the most powerful aspects of selling on the internet using an e-commerce website is that in addition to using well-written text, referred to as *copy*, to advertise, describe, and promote your offerings and to educate consumers about them, you can also use eye-catching photographs, colorful graphic images, sounds, music, video, graphic animations, as well as other interactive multimedia elements and content.

CREATING A PERCEIVED NEED

Learning how to create a perceived need or demand for a product/service is a skill and an art form that writers, hosts (that is, pitchmen), and producers of television infomercials and televised shopping networks have mastered. As you begin to acquire these skills for yourself, learn from the masters by watching infomercials on TV. You'll quickly begin wondering how you've ever lived without whatever the pitchman is selling and probably feel yourself being compelled to call the toll-free number to place an order. It's that sense of importance, excitement, urgency, and craving that you want to create when you begin to promote and sell your products/services on your website.

The internet is interactive, which makes it potentially a far more powerful selling tool than a traditional and passive (non-interactive) newspaper or magazine ad, television commercial, billboard, or radio commercial, for example. Just because a wide range of online-based elements can be used to expertly sell your products/services online, remember they must be used effectively to have an impact on your customer. Having a bunch of flashy bells and whistles on a website may look amazing, but if that makes your site confusing to navigate or says little or nothing about what you're actually selling, they are virtually useless.

Discovering the best ways to harness the power of the internet and design a professional-looking website that caters to your target audience is covered in Chapter 7. However, before you can design your website and launch your advertising campaign to promote your products/services and your site, you must first understand exactly whom you're trying to reach and then determine the best approach for effectively reaching them.

Properly Reaching Your Customers and Driving Them to Your Website

During your website's design phase, it's essential that every element and piece of content incorporated into your site to cater to your target audience. Just because you have the ability to add flashy add-ons to your site by using graphic animations, sound effects, and other elements, you should not use them unless they help you quickly and effectively communicate your sales message and create a demand for what you're selling. A professional-looking website doesn't have to be complex in order to achieve its objectives. In fact, more often than not, from a design standpoint, simple, straightforward, easy-to-understand, and simple-to-navigate is better and more effective as a sales tool.

Likewise, as you begin to market your products and drive traffic to your site, you'll want to use proven and cost-efficient marketing, advertising, public relations, and promotional methods that you believe your target audience will relate to and, more importantly, respond to favorably. Consumers are bombarded by advertising messages everywhere, virtually every waking hour of the day. They see and hear advertising messages on TV, on the radio, in print ads, on billboards, in junk mail in online advertising, and on T-shirts and apparel worn by everyday people. Everyone is accustomed to tuning these messages out.

It's become that much more difficult for someone trying to market and sell a product or service to capture the attention of a target audience, especially in a low-cost, efficient way. Because you probably can't afford to launch a multimillion dollar television campaign to drive traffic to your website, you need to find innovative, creative, and affordable ways to capture the attention of your target audience, create a demand for your products/services, and get those people to place orders.

As an online business operator, one of your goals should be to become an expert at low-cost, grassroots marketing techniques that allow you to reach that niche audience comprised specifically of people be interested in what you're selling.

Analyzing Your Competition

Before opening for business, go online and determine who your competition is for whatever products or services you plan to offer. Figure out your competition's approach to marketing, pricing, servicing its customers, and utilizing its online presence, and then figure out what you will do differently to set yourself apart and do things better in order to be competitive in the market-place.

While anyone or any business can always compete by offering lower pricing than the competition, this is seldom the best approach to take, especially in a highly competitive industry. Instead, focus on what you can do better and what value-added services you can offer to justify premium pricing and create a demand for your superior products/services. Offering value-added services or add-ons to products can be very attractive to customers and help them justify the expense of what you're selling. Be creative, so that whatever it is you're doing to add value to your offerings is something your target customers want, need, and will appreciate.

If you'll be doing custom work for clients as a website designer, graphic artist, or photographer, you'll quickly discover that many clients are willing to pay a bit extra for guaranteed top-notch customer service and to hire someone they know is a recognized expert with proven experience. Develop a reputation for meeting deadlines, offering reliable service, sticking to price estimates, and providing highly professional and top-quality products and services. Whatever your competition is doing, figure out how you can do it better and make these strategies part of your initial business plan.

As you begin working with potential clients, you should be able to intelligently discuss why what you're offering is better than your competition and show that you fully understand what your competition does. This allows you to address specific questions from your prospective customers/clients about why they should hire you as opposed to your competition. This reasoning can

CLICK TIP

Analyzing your competition is an ongoing process. An in-depth analysis of your competition should be done before launching your own business, and then redone on a regular basis so you stay on the cutting-edge and in the know. When a new competitor pops up, you want to learn as much as possible about them quickly. When any of your competitors fail, you'll want to analyze what they did wrong and learn from their mistakes.

be included in your own website's online content and marketing materials, but should be supported with samples of your very best work showcased in your online portfolio.

Working as a Startup Versus Someone with Plenty of Real-World Experience

Unless you already have years worth of real-world experience working with high-profile clientele, you'll need to rely on your raw talent and ability to market your "potential" using grassroots marketing, advertising, and public relations techniques when you're first starting out as a freelance website designer, graphic artist, or photographer doing business on the web. As someone just starting out, your online portfolio might not be extensive. Yet it must be highly professional looking and truly showcase your potential, allowing your customers/clients to overlook your lack of proven experience.

As you'll learn in Chapter 9, there are many ways those starting out can enhance their portfolio, for example, by volunteering your services to charitable organizations. Volunteering allows you to do work for credible and potentially high-profile clients, build up your portfolio, and gain real world experience.

Launching a new business or branching out as a self-employed freelancer means taking on a wide range of additional responsibilities beyond doing the revenue-generating work for your clients or simply selling your products/services. Chapter 4 will help you prepare to successfully take on these additional responsibilities.

Those who already have vast experience working in their field and who simply want to develop an online presence to increase their customer base typically rely on word-of-mouth advertising from present and past clients and customers and do not have to spend much time or money on paid advertising, marketing, or public relations. Ultimately, this is the position you want to be in.

Chapter 3

Putting Together Your Professional Toolbox

A lot goes into launching your own business, especially if you're planning to both launch an online component to your business and begin work as an independent freelancer. If you've worked in your desired field as an employee for another company, you already have many of the professional skills, plus the knowledge and experience do to your work, but you might not have the skills and knowledge needed to be your own boss, operate your own company, and achieve success as an independent freelancer. This chapter focuses on what it takes to be self-employed and operate your online business, and it explores what business-related tools and resources you'll need to get started.

Are You Cut Out for Self-Employment?

Being self-employed can be summed up in just four words: You are the boss! With this job title, however, comes a tremendous amount of responsibility and it requires additional skills that are not typically required of someone who works for someone else's company. For example, as the boss you'll need to make many important decisions on an ongoing basis about how your business is operated. There's nobody looking over your shoulder, and you have nobody to answer to. You're responsible for handling your finances including all bookkeeping and accounting as well as for managing your customers, clients, and employees.

As the wearer of many hats, marketing, advertising, and public relations also fall into your realm of responsibilities, as do building and maintaining relationships with vendors and suppliers, budgeting your time and resources, and handling your day-to-day work as a freelance professional.

The more business-related knowledge and experience you have, the better off you'll be as you start out. Even with previous business experience, however, be prepared to invest a significant amount of time, money, and resources in planning, managing, and growing all aspects of your business, plus operating your online presence.

You must have the skills necessary to look at the big picture, make important business decisions that will impact your short-term and long-term success, have the ability to properly manage your finances, and always be working to grow your business. You'll also need to know when it's necessary to hire outside experts to help you with tasks you're simply not qualified to handle yourself.

Self-employment means having to juggle many unrelated tasks simultaneously,: working under tight deadlines, making important decisions, and paying careful attention to detail. All of these skills are essential. Many of the

SEEK HELP WHEN IT'S NEEDED

Even if you have all of the skills, knowledge, and experience to be a successful website designer, graphic artist, or photographer to work as an independent freelancer, there will be business-related tasks and responsibilities you might not have the knowledge or experience to handle properly. In these situations, the best thing you can do is hire freelance professionals to help you out. Typical outside experts are a freelance bookkeeper or accountant to help with financial matters, a lawyer to help with the legal aspects of establishing your business, or various marketing, advertising, and/or public relations specialists who can help you properly promote your business. Remember, being the boss does not mean you have to do everything yourself, even initially.

additional business-related skills you want and need can be acquired on an as-needed basis by reading how-to books, taking classes, learning from experts you hire, and from trial and error on the job. The problem with taking this last approach is that you're more apt to make mistakes that could be time consuming and extremely costly to fix. As you experience the learning curve associated with launching your own business, your goal should be to learn as much as possible before you get started, anticipate what mistakes could be made in advance, and then develop plans for avoiding them. Have a game plan for successfully and efficiently dealing with obstacles and challenges as they arise—and they will.

While you may be an amazingly talented website designer, graphic artist, or photographer, you may not have the skills, desire, or fortitude to handle everything else involved with being your own boss, operating your own business, and being in absolute control of your professional destiny. Not everyone is cut out for this, so it's essential that you understand exactly what you're getting into, what responsibilities you'll be taking on, what additional stresses you'll have to deal with, and what sacrifices you'll need to make in your personal life in order to plan, launch, operate, and grow your business.

> ## WARNING
>
> Realistically, at least for the first 6 to 12 months of your business's operation, the time commitment involved will be significantly greater than you initially anticipate. And it's essential that the financial projections incorporated into your business plan be accurate. These financial forecasts must allow for enough startup capital and operational funds to keep the business running for up to 12 months, or however long it takes for you to generate enough revenue to support the business and yourself financially. As a startup business, don't forget to calculate the need for funds to properly market and promote your business.

The Pros and Cons of Self-Employment

There are advantages and disadvantages associated with being your own boss and working as an independent freelancer, just as there are to operating your business primarily online, as opposed to from a storefront or traditional office.

Some of the benefits to working as an independent, self-employed freelancer and online business operator include:

- ➡ You're your own boss and have nobody to answer to.
- ➡ You can make your own decisions and have total control over your professional destiny.
- ➡ You can set your own work schedule.
- ➡ You can pursue whatever professional interests you have and select your own area of expertise or specialty.
- ➡ You have the ability to take on only the clients you want and/or choose what products you wish to sell.
- ➡ You can decide if you wish to work with clients solely through the internet or if you wish to work with them in person.
- ➡ You set all of your own prices and determine your own value in the marketplace.
- ➡ Your earning potential is limited only by how hard you work and your ability to continuously generate new business while soliciting repeat business from past and present clients/customers.

➡ You have the ability to hire and fire employees or utilize subcontractors or other freelancers to help you with bigger jobs or projects.

➡ You can work from home.

➡ There are significant tax benefits to being self-employed and working from your own home. Be sure to consult with an accountant so you can take full advantage of these benefits and incentives, which could save you thousands of dollars per year.

Some of the potential drawbacks to being your own boss and operating your own business include:

➡ You'll need to juggle many business-related tasks simultaneously, including responsibilities that fall outside of working as a website designer, graphic artist, or photographer, tasks such as accounting/bookkeeping, marketing, website management, and client/customer relations.

➡ You control your own financial destiny. If you make a mistake or mismanage your funds, your business and your personal finances could be put in jeopardy.

➡ Because the time commitment is significant, it will often require making sacrifices in your personal life.

➡ You'll need to learn and utilize many skills that may not currently be part of your professional skill set.

➡ You are solely responsible for building up and maintaining your professional reputation. If anything happens to your reputation as a result of a mistake or mismanagement of a client, for example, the negative and long-term repercussions could be significant.

➡ You are responsible for supplying your own work-related benefits, including all types of insurance. This can be costly for a self-employed professional, especially if benefits are needed for multiple family members.

➡ Depending on your business model, you will only generate revenue, and income, if you're working. Thus, there will be no such thing as a paid vacation.

➡ You'll need to do things better than your competition and find ways to stand out and set yourself apart in the marketplace.

NEED A PARTNER?

After evaluating all that goes into launching and operating your own business and working as a freelance professional, you may determine you're not yet ready to handle the responsibilities alone. Perhaps you consider yourself more of a creative individual than a businessperson. Before abandoning the idea of launching your own business, consider the benefits of taking on one or more business partners who are more experienced or knowledgeable about business operations and who are willing to share some of the financial risk associated with launching a business.

Another option is to accept a full- or part-time job for another company or agency and use this experience to perfect your skills so you'll one day be more qualified to handle the responsibilities involved with being your own boss and be more confident in your abilities.

If you're not 100 percent prepared to invest the necessary time and money for launching your own business and you don't have the confidence needed to achieve success, don't pursue this opportunity until you're completely ready. It's perfectly normal to be nervous about making such a life-changing decision, even knowing you have the qualifications and confidence to make it work. It's another thing altogether to go into a new business venture totally unprepared.

How an Online Business Differs from Traditional Retail

While a traditional retail store can sell the same products as an online website, there are major differences between operating a traditional brick-and-mortar retail store and an online e-commerce operation. There are also differences between opening up an office and working as an independent freelancer from home. Some of the costs and drawbacks associated with operating a traditional brick-and-mortar business, that is, a storefront or office, include

➡ having to purchase, lease, or rent the retail and/or office space (at a cost of hundreds or thousands of dollars per month).

➡ the need to hire employees and managers to staff your **store** and/or run your office.

➡ having to purchase and maintain plenty of inventory (if you're operating a store).

➡ having to purchase store fixtures and displays, and items such as point-of-sale merchandising materials, signage, cash registers, and/or office furniture and equipment.

➡ remaining open during pre-defined operating hours.

➡ being in a fixed location and typically only attracting customers within a specific geographic area or region.

➡ incurring costs in the tens of thousands or hundreds of thousands of dollars—sometimes more.

➡ competing with mass-market retailers and chain stores in local markets.

➡ assuming the tremendous risk involved in opening a traditional retail store or office as a startup business.

On the other hand, operating an online-based business offers a wide range of benefits, including

➡ very low startup and overhead costs.

➡ a potentially worldwide customer base.

➡ the ability to accept orders and promote your products/services 24-hours-per-day, 365-days-per-year, because your website is always open and available to web surfers.

➡ a flexible work schedule.

➡ smaller inventory requirements.

➡ the ability to operate from almost anywhere, such as from within your home or a small office/warehouse location.

➡ the relative ease of one person createing a website that's as professional looking as a site operated by a large, well-established, multimillion dollar company, thus leveling the playing field.

➡ a website can be created and open for business in hours or days, not months or even years.

➡ very low financial risk (in the hundreds or thousands of dollars, sometimes less).

➡ the ability to sell virtually any product that can be sold in a traditional retail environment.

➡ the easy sale of downloadables and/or services.

Free Online Resources

Before taking on the risks and responsibilities of self-employment, make sure you have what it'll take to be successful. In addition to reading the interviews featured later in this book, it will be extremely helpful for you to seek out other self-employed professionals so you can learn from their experiences and develop realistic expectations. If you don't know anyone else working as a freelance professional, consider joining one or more professional organizations and your local chamber of commerce, or soliciting the free support offered by SCORE, a nonprofit association dedicated to educating entrepreneurs in the formation, growth, and success of small business nationwide. SCORE is a resource partner with the U.S. Small Business Administration. To receive free guidance and support visit score.org or call (800) 634-0245.

The Entrepreneur.com website (entrepreneur.com) is an excellent resource for startup business operators. From the website, click on the "Grow Your Business," "E-Business," and/or "Entrepreneur Assist" icon located on the homepage. The Federal Citizens Information Center (888-878-3256/pueblo.gsa.gov) is also an excellent resource for startup business operators and people looking to branch out and become freelance professionals. From this website, you can download dozens of informative brochures and guides that will help you acquire the additional business and financial knowledge

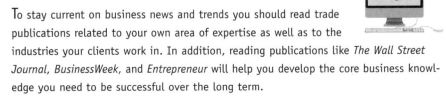

CLICK TIP

To stay current on business news and trends you should read trade publications related to your own area of expertise as well as to the industries your clients work in. In addition, reading publications like *The Wall Street Journal, BusinessWeek,* and *Entrepreneur* will help you develop the core business knowledge you need to be successful over the long term.

you'll need to be successful. From the website's homepage, click on the "Small Business" icon that's located on the left side of the screen.

The Small Business Administration's website (sba.gov/smallbusiness planner/index.html) is another information-packed resource available free of charge to those interested in launching their own business. The website offers tools and resources for creating a business plan, acquiring financing, selecting an appropriate business structure, managing your business, and dealing with tax-related issues pertaining to being self-employed.

Professional Tools You'll Need to Get Started

As you create your business's startup budget, consider the core tools you'll need to effectively do your creative work as well as those needed to create and manage your online presence and handle the day-to-day tasks associated with operating your business. From a technology standpoint, you'll need to acquire one or more computers, scanners, digital cameras, printers, graphic tablets, and other peripherals, along with specialized software for website design, graphic arts, and photography. You'll definitely want the latest versions of the software you'll be using on a daily basis to do your creative work, whether it's Adobe Dreamweaver for website design, Adobe Photoshop to edit graphics and photos, or Adobe Illustrator to do graphic design work.

Chapter 4 offers a more comprehensive list of business-related tools you'll need to launch your business. Now is also a good time

> **CLICK TIP**
>
>
>
> Adobe Creative Suite 3 Master Collection for PC or Mac (MSRP: $2,500, adobe.com/products/creative suite/mastercollection) offers a complete collection of all of Adobe's bestselling programs for website design, graphic arts, and photography, in one package.

to start researching internet service providers (ISPs) to host your business's online presence and provide you with access to the web. If you'll be providing website development services for clients, you might want to establish a relationship with an ISP so you can bundle website hosting with your creative services.

Setting Up Your Business Infrastructure

*M*oving forward and launching an online business and/or choosing to work as an independent freelancer is a huge decision. Once you determine you have what it takes to be successful and have developed a business plan based on the business model you're planning to pursue, you need to establish the infrastructure for your business and create a legal business entity.

If you know you want to pursue this type of opportunity but haven't yet selected the business model that will generate adequate revenue to meet your personal, financial, and business goals, Chapter 6 will teach you about the various business models and opportunities available to skilled website designers, graphic artists, and photographers who wish to establish an online-based business.

Getting Professional Help

Depending on where you'll be doing business, local laws and regulations vary greatly. As you move forward, consider sitting down with an attorney who has experience helping local entrepreneurs establish their business ventures to make sure all of the necessary licenses and permits are acquired and the required paperwork is completed correctly.

As you already know, starting an online business is like starting any other type of business. To do this correctly, you have to follow the letter of the law. A few of the legal and financial issues that you will need to deal with include:

- Registering a business name and internet URL
- Selecting a legal business structure
- Obtaining a business license
- Obtaining a sales tax ID number
- Acquiring appropriate insurance
- Establishing a company bank account
- Preparing and filing business and income tax returns

Investing the funds necessary to seek out professional legal and financial (accounting) advice is money well spent, as the guidance you obtain from these people will not only help you avoid costly mistakes but also will assist you in properly establishing your business venture.

Lawyers with small business experience are able to advise you on which legal business structure best meets your needs as well as review with you related insurance and liability issues. Your lawyer can also draft necessary legal documents, create or review your supplier and vendor agreements, and help you address other important legal issues.

The lawyer(s) you hire, at least initially, can help you decipher the legalese associated with starting a new business and make sense of complicated issues pertaining to that business. Likewise, working with an accountant can help you decipher the sometimes complicated financial information you must know in order to comply with state and federal tax regulations.

Depending on your level of expertise and previous experience operating a business, it may only be necessary to hire a lawyer and/or accountant for a few hours as you get your business up and running. Once your business is fully operational, however, you'll also want a lawyer and accountant at your disposal when a question or need for their services arise. Having an established relationship with a lawyer and accountant can ultimately save you time, aggravation, and money.

To obtain a referral for a competent and experienced lawyer, consider contacting your state's bar association. A referral for an accountant can be obtained by contacting your state's board of accountancy. If, however, you can obtain a personal referral from someone you know, that too can be a wise strategy.

Legal Business Structure Options

When establishing an online-based business that will also involve you doing in-person freelance work for your clients, it's important to select the proper business structure to meet your unique needs. Your primary choices for a business designed to earn a profit (as opposed to a non-profit organization) are:

- ➡ a corporation,
- ➡ a limited liability corporation,
- ➡ a partnership, or
- ➡ sole proprietorship (or DBA).

Issues such as budget, tax implications, and personal liability as a business operator are determining factors when selecting a business structure. This is a decision your lawyer and/or accountant can help you make.

Initially, many people choose a sole proprietorship, also referred to as a DBA or "doing business as," if they are on a tight budget and comfortable with the liability issues associated with this form of business. It is the easiest and least expensive business to establish. A partnership is the right choice if you will be running your new business with a spouse, family member, friend, or a business partner. A limited liability corporation (LLC) or corporation is the appropriate choice if your plans include expansion and you want to minimize personal liability concerns. There are also different tax liability issues associated with each of these business entities. Some of the advantages and disadvantages of each are discussed later in this chapter.

Regardless of the legal structure you adopt for your business venture, you need to select and register a business name. The name you choose can incorporate your own name, such as "John Doe's Website Design," or it can be a made up name, such as "Acme Photography." The key is to come up with a name that's unique and that does not violate another company's trademark(s) or copyrights.

Have two or three name options ready to go in case another business is already using your first choice. Business registration costs vary by state and province, though generally this one-time fee is less than $200 if you're registering a sole proprietorship. Your lawyer can assist you with this process, or you can file the necessary forms yourself with local and/or state governments.

> ### CLICK TIP
>
>
>
> **At** the same time you select your business name, make sure the website URL (website address) is available and can be registered. Information on how to do this can be found in Chapter 6.

Normally, you have to show proof of business registration in order to establish a company bank account, buy products wholesale, obtain a business loan, and/or secure a credit card merchant account.

The following resources will help you find an attorney and register your business with the proper government authorities:

- ➥ American Bar Association: (202) 662-1000, abanet.org
- ➥ Canadian Bar Association: (800) 267-8860, cba.org
- ➥ Canadian Business Service Centers (Small-business registration services and information): (888) 576-4444, cbsc.org
- ➥ Canadian Corp. Online Filing: canadiancorp.com
- ➥ Small Business Administration (SBA): (800) U-ASK-SBA, sba.gov
- ➥ National Association of State Boards of Accountancy (NASBA): nasba.org

The Sole Proprietorship

A sole proprietorship is the most common type of legal business structure, mainly because it is the simplest and least expensive to start and maintain. A sole proprietorship means your business entity and your personal affairs are merged together as one. For example, you'll file a single state and federal tax return, and take on personal liability for all accrued business debts and actions (including legal actions). You personally control all revenues and profits.

Even if you're operating a sole proprietorship, it's important to separate your business finances from your personal finances for record-keeping and income tax purposes. For instance, interest payments on credit cards used for business purchases are tax-deductible, while interest payments on personal credit cards (used for personal purchases) are not.

Perhaps the biggest advantage of sole proprietorships is that they are very simple to form and can be started, altered, bought, sold, or closed at any time, quickly and inexpensively. Also, other than obtaining routine business registrations, permits, and licenses, there are few government regulations.

The biggest disadvantage of a sole proprietorship is that you are 100 percent legally and financially liable for any number of business activities that could go wrong. As a result, all of your personal assets, including investments and real estate, could be lost as a direct result of generating too much business-related debt or successful litigation against you or your business.

Partnership

A partnership is another low-cost legal business structure. It allows two or more people to start, operate, and own a business. If you opt to start a business with a family member, friend, or business partner, make sure the partnership is based on a written partnership agreement, not just a verbal one. (Again, this is a topic to discuss with your attorney.)

Your partnership agreement should be a legally binding document that addresses a variety of issues, such as financial investment, profit distribution, the duties of each partner, and an exit strategy should one partner want out of the agreement later. The absence of a formal agreement can be extremely problematic should disagreements arise that cannot be resolved (which is a very common occurrence) or should one of the partners unexpectedly die or want out of the business. Like a sole proprietorship, business profits are split among partners proportionate to their ownership and are treated as taxable personal income.

One potential advantage of a partnership is that all financial and legal risks, as well as the work associated with operating the business, is shared by more than one person. This allows each partner to take on specific tasks based on their area of expertise in order to benefit the collective team. Record-keeping requirements are basic and on a par with a sole proprietorship.

Unfortunately, partnerships also have disadvantages. The most significant is that each partner is legally responsible and personally liable for the other partners' actions in the business. It's important to understand that a nonincorporated partnership offers no legal protection from liability or financial issues. All partners are equally responsible for the business's debts, liabilities, and actions.

The Limited Liability Corporation (LLC)

A limited liability corporation combines many of the characteristics of a corporation with those of a partnership. Like a corporation, an LLC provides protection from personal liabilities, but the tax advantages of a partnership are associated with it. An LLC can be formed by one or more people. These people, alone or together, organize a legal entity that's separate and distinct from each owner's personal affairs in most legal and financial respects.

There are multiple advantages of a limited liability corporation (over a corporation or partnership). For example, an LLC is less expensive to form and maintain than a corporation, and this business entity offers protection from personal liability, which partnerships do not provide. There are also simplified taxation and reporting rules associated with an LLC (compared to a corporation). Because of these advantages, limited liability corporations have become the fastest-growing form of business structure in the United States.

To determine if forming an LLC is appropriate for your business, seriously consider consulting with an attorney and/or accountant who specializes in these matters.

Corporation

The most complicated business structure for a startup business is the corporation. When you form a corporation, you create a legal entity that is totally separate and distinct from the shareholders of the corporation as well as the business's owners/operators. Because the corporation becomes its own entity, it assumes debt and can legally sue or be sued, and as a tax-paying entity, must pay taxes on its taxable income (profit) prior to paying any dividends to the shareholders. The corporation's finances and financial records are completely separate from the finances of its shareholders and operators.

The biggest advantage to incorporating your business is that you can greatly reduce your own personal liability. Because a corporation is its own entity, it can legally borrow money and be held accountable in a number of matters from a legal standpoint. In effect, this releases you from most personal and financial liability. The major disadvantage is double taxation. Corporation profits are taxed, and then the same profits are taxed again in the form of personal income tax when distributed to the shareholders as a dividend. Unfortunately, the same does not hold true if the corporation loses money. Financial losses cannot be used as a personal income tax deduction for shareholders.

Forming a corporation is a relatively quick process. However, this process varies by state. In addition to a filing fee, there are annual fees, as well as annual state and federal tax liabilities associated with operating a corporation, whether or not it is profitable. Your attorney will be able to help you establish a corporation if it's deemed appropriate, or you can file the paperwork yourself. For a fee, several online-based services, such as Incorporate Fast (incorporatefast.com), Legal Zoom (legalzoom.com), My Corporation (mycorporation.com), and The Company Corporation (incorporate.com) allow you to set up your own corporation in minutes.

Licenses

All businesses must be licensed. In fact, chances are you will to need to obtain several licenses and permits, depending on the type of product you sell, how the product is sold, and where you do business. Don't even think about skipping any of the required licenses and permits! At the very least, this could result in huge fines. Depending on what laws you break, it could also be a criminal offense and result in imprisonment.

At minimum, you need a business license, vendor's permits, and a resale certificate or sales tax permit ID number. Additional permits and licenses that may be needed include a health permit if you sell food, a police clearance certificate if you sell home-security products, and an import and export certificate if you bring products into the country or ship products out. A home-occupation permit is required to work from home in some states as is a building permit if you significantly alter your home to suit your new business venture.

Licenses are also necessary simply to be a business. They are validation. You probably need a license or permit to buy wholesale, open commercial bank accounts, and obtain a credit card merchant account.

Business License

To legally operate a business in all municipalities of the United States and Canada, you need to obtain a business license. Business license costs vary depending on your geographic location, expected sales, and the type of business or products you'll be selling.

Because these licenses are issued at the municipal level, contact your city/county clerk's or permits' office for the full requirements for a business license. The Small Business Administration (SBA) also provides a directory, indexed by state, outlining where business licenses can be obtained. This directory is located at sba.gov/hotlist/license.html.

Additionally, in the United States and Canada, you can also contact your local chamber of commerce to inquire about business license requirements and fees. Check your local phone book or Yellow Pages for a listing.

Permits

What permits are called sometimes varies, based on your geographic location, but whatever you want to call it, you need a permit to collect and remit sales tax. Common terms used include *resale certificate*, *sales tax permit*, or *tax ID number*.

Almost all states and provinces now impose a sales tax on products sold directly to consumers or end users. It is the business owner's responsibility to collect and remit these sales taxes. The same sales tax permits are needed when purchasing goods for resale from manufacturers and wholesalers so the goods can be bought tax-free. (Ultimately, the tax will be paid by the retail customers when the items are later resold.)

The SBA provides a directory, indexed by state, outlining where and how sales tax permits and/or ID numbers may be obtained, including information on completing and remitting sales tax forms. This directory is located at sba.gov/hotlist/license.html. In Canada there are two levels of sales tax. The first is charged by most provinces on the sale of retail products to consumers, and the second is charged by the federal government. The latter is known as the *goods and services* tax and is charged on the retail sale of all goods and most services. You can obtain a Federal Goods and Services Sales/Harmonized Sales Tax (GST/HST) number by contacting the Canada Customs and Revenue Agency (ccra-adrc.gc.ca).

Insurance

Just as people utilize health insurance, homeowner's insurance, automobile insurance, life insurance, and dental insurance to help protect them financially, business also requires insurance. As a business operator, what types of insurance you require depends on several factors, including what you'll be selling, how and where you'll be storing your inventory (if applicable), who you'll be selling to, and where you'll be conducting your business. The business insurance you acquire also protects your personal assets.

Invest the time to meet with an insurance company representative or broker to help you review your current personal insurance coverage and determine what additional business-related coverage is required. To further protect yourself personally, you might also investigate purchasing an umbrella insurance policy that offers at least $1 million dollars of additional coverage.

Step one is to choose an insurance agent or broker who is familiar with the specific insurance needs of the small-business owner. Not only will the agent be able to translate insurance legalese into easily understandable, plain English for you, but he will also be able to find the best coverage for your individual needs and at the lowest cost. Be sure to shop around and get quotes from at least three different insurance providers.

There is a plethora of business insurances available for every imaginable contingency, but the coverage you'll definitely require as a business operator is property and liability insurance. For more information about finding an insurance broker, contact the Independent Insurance Agents and Brokers of America's website at iiaa.org or the Insurance Brokers Association of Canada's website at ibac.ca.

Property Insurance

Because some entrepreneurs operate or manage their business from home, property insurance, which generally covers buildings and contents, is your first line of protection.

Depending on how extensive your property insurance is, it may provide protection in the form of a cash settlement or paid repairs in the event of fire, theft, vandalism, flood, earthquake, wind damage, acts of God, and malicious damage.

Property insurance is the starting point from which you should branch out to include specialized tools and equipment, inventory, and other liability riders, depending on the types of products and services you'll be selling. Contacting your insurance agent and asking questions specific to your business, equipment, and inventory will quickly reveal what is or is not covered by your existing policy.

In most cases, you will want to increase the value of the contents' portion if you use expensive computer and office equipment. You also want to insure cash on hand, accounts receivable records, and inventory, which will require a special rider added to your basic insurance policy.

Liability Insurance

Most homeowners have some sort of liability protection built into their basic homeowner's insurance policy. This is also true of people who rent, because landlords are obligated by law in most places to carry property and liability insurance on rented buildings and land.

No matter how diligent you are in terms of taking all necessary precautions to protect any person or customer by removing potential hazards from your home, property, business, and products, you could still be held legally responsible for events beyond your control. The best protection against this is liability insurance coverage.

This type of extended liability insurance is often referred to as general business liability or umbrella business liability. General business liability coverage insures a business against accidents and injury that might occur at the home, at a customer's location, retailing venues, or other perils related to the products you sell. It provides protection from the costs associated with successful litigation or claims against your business or you, depending on the legal entity of your business, and covers such things as medical expenses, recovery expenses, property damage, and other costs typically associated with liability situations.

Even if your business is not directly involved in manufacturing the products you sell, you still must be proactive in terms of product liability insurance concerns. In litigation situations, it is not uncommon for plaintiffs who have suffered damages as a result of product malfunction to name numerous defendants in their claim, including the product retailer.

Health and Long-Term Disability Insurance

If you'll be operating your business venture on a full-time basis and it will represent your entire income, consider investing in health as well as long-term disability insurance. Health insurance will cover your medical bills if you become ill or get injured. What happens, however, if due to a long-term illness or injury, you're unable to work for three months, six months, one year, or longer? What would happen to your personal financial situation if you no longer had an income and were unable to work? This is where long-term disability insurance kicks in. Obtaining this type of policy involves additional cost, but it can save you from total financial ruin in a medical emergency.

How Much Money Do You Need to Launch Your Online Business?

Another important consideration is how much money you need to start your online business. The amount needed depends on the type of products and services you are planning to sell, as well as other factors such as transportation, marketing, advertising, and equipment requirements. Some people already have many of the things needed to operate their business, while others must purchase or rent these items. The following worksheet (Figure 4.1) will help you calculate how much money will be needed to start your business. This is just one of the financial projections you'll ultimately want to incorporate into your comprehensive business plan.

If this is your first foray into the world of business ownership, you should know that in addition to startup capital, you will also need working capital. This is the money needed to keep the business operational until it becomes profitable. Again, depending on what you're selling, and a variety of other factors, this could take several months or up to a year or longer.

Startup capital is needed to purchase equipment and office furniture, to meet legal requirements, to pay for training, and to purchase initial inventory. Working capital is needed to pay bills (for your company as well as for yourself), until the business generates revenues and profits and becomes self-sufficient.

Figure 4.1: **STARTUP COSTS WORKSHEET**

Use this handy worksheet to calculate how much money you will need to start your online business. Ignore items not relevant to your business, and add items as required.

Business Setup

Business registration	$ _____
Business license	$ _____
Vendor's permits	$ _____
Other permits	$ _____
Insurance	$ _____
Professional fees	$ _____
Training/education	$ _____
Bank account	$ _____

Figure 4.1: **STARTUP COSTS WORKSHEET,** continued

Business Setup (cont.)

Merchant accounts $ _____

Payment processing equipment $ _____

Association fees $ _____

Deposits $ _____

Other _____ $ _____

Subtotal A $ _____

Business Identity

Business cards $ _____

Logo design $ _____

Letterhead $ _____

Envelopes $ _____

Other _____ $ _____

Subtotal B $ _____

Office Setup

Computer hardware $ _____

Communication equipment $ _____

Software $ _____

Furniture $ _____

Other office equipment $ _____

Office supplies $ _____

Office renovations $ _____

Other _____ $ _____

Subtotal C $ _____

Figure 4.1: **STARTUP COSTS WORKSHEET,** continued

Transportation

Cost to buy/lease transportation	$ _____
Registration	$ _____
Insurance	$ _____
Moving equipment	$ _____
Shipping/delivery supplies	$ _____
Other _____	$ _____
Subtotal D	$ _____

Website Creation and Launch

Domain registration	$ _____
Site development fees	$ _____
Search engine/directory fees	$ _____
Equipment	$ _____
Software	$ _____
Content creation	$ _____
Website hosting (ISP)	$ _____
e-commerce Turnkey Solution	$ _____
Other _____	$ _____
Subtotal E	$ _____

Marketing

Research and planning costs	$ _____
Signage	$ _____
Brochures/fliers (design/printing)	$ _____
Catalogs (design/printing)	$ _____
Initial advertising budget	$ _____
Initial online promotion budget	$ _____

Figure 4.1: **STARTUP COSTS WORKSHEET,** continued

Marketing

Search engine optimization budget $ _____

Search engine marketing budget $ _____

Public relations budget $ _____

Other _____ $ _____

    Subtotal F $ _____

Merchandising

Product samples $ _____

Pricing/value guides $ _____

Display racks/cases $ _____

Kiosks/carts $ _____

Portable booth/display/kiosk $_____

Other _____ $ _____

    Subtotal G $ _____

Inventory

a. _____ $ _____

b. _____ $ _____

c. _____ $ _____

d. _____ $ _____

e. _____ $ _____

    Subtotal H $ _____

Adding Up the Costs

Subtotal A $ _____

Subtotal B $ _____

Subtotal C $ _____

Figure 4.1: **STARTUP COSTS WORKSHEET,** continued

Adding Up the Costs

Subtotal D $ _____

Subtotal E $ _____

Subtotal F $ _____

Subtotal G $ _____

Subtotal H $ _____

Total Startup Costs $ _____

Working Capital(*) $ _____

Total Investment Needed $ _____

(*) With the help of your accountant, perform financial projections based on 3, 6, 12, 18, and 24 months.

Acquiring the Funds

Knowing you need funds to get started, the next logical question is where is this money coming from? Well, you have several options:

→ Personal savings
→ Loans from family or friends
→ Bank loans
→ Government loans (small business loans)
→ Credit cards
→ Investor or investors
→ Social lending services

Personal Savings

The fastest and simplest way to finance your new business is right from your own bank account, especially if the investment is small and manageable. Self-financing means you do not have to worry about applying for a loan, accumulating unnecessary debt, or paying interest on borrowed money.

You can use your personal savings, cash in an investment certificate, or use retirement funds, mutual funds, stocks, or insurance policies. Keep in mind, however, that money you remove from fixed certificates or retirement investments may be subject to additional personal income tax or specific penalties for early withdrawal or cancellation.

Be sure to consult with a financial planner before cashing, selling, or redeeming any investment or certificates. Also, depending on the investment you want to liquidate, you might actually be earning a higher rate of return than the interest rate you can secure for a business startup loan.

One innovative way to fund your venture is to create a list of all personal items you no longer want or need and sell them by holding a garage sale, using eBay.com, or renting a flea market booth. Not only can this raise the money needed to get started, but you also gain valuable sales experience in the process and clear your home of unwanted junk.

Borrowing from Family and Friends

If you don't have the necessary startup capital yourself, another potential source is to borrow money from friends or family. This type of funding is often referred to as a *love loan*. There is a potential downside to this tactic, however. First, as an "investor," your friend or relative may feel entitled to offer you unsolicited advice and criticism about how you run your business. Also, if your business fails, will you be able to pay back the money you borrow? If not, your relationship could be damaged beyond repair. Still, many extremely successful business ventures have been built on money borrowed from friends and family members.

If you decide to borrow from friends or family to fund your business, treat the transaction as you would if you were borrowing the money from a bank. Have a promissory note drawn up and signed, noting all the details—principal loan amount, interest, and repayment dates. Whatever you do, make sure you stick to your repayment schedule to avoid disputes.

VirginMoney.com (800-805-2472) is a relatively new service that facilitates the borrowing (or lending) of money between friends and family members. By acting as an independent and unbiased middleman for a small fee, Virgin Money.com helps establish the terms of the loan, then creates the necessary paperwork and manages the loan. Having this formal agreement in place protects both parties and eliminates the chance of confusion or misunderstandings.

Bank Loans (Small Business Loans)

If you have good credit (a personal FICO credit score higher than 650), you can apply for a small business or startup loan from a bank or credit union. The loan can be secured, meaning it is guaranteed with some other type of investment, such as a guaranteed investment certificate, or it can be unsecured, with the funds advanced because of your credit worthiness.

Secured loans have lower interest rates, by as much as 5 percent. Another option is to talk to your banker about setting up a line of credit. Secured lines of credit also enjoy lower interest rates than unsecured credit lines. One advantage of a line of credit over a standard business loan is that most only require you to repay interest based on the account balance, and not on the entire principal and interest.

For example, a $10,000 line of credit fully extended with a per annum interest rate of 5 percent would require minimum monthly payments of $41.66 ($10,000 multiplied by 5 percent divided by 12 months = $41.66). Of course, this is interest repayment only, and you would not be paying down the principal amount. But this flexibility provides exactly the kind of breathing room new business ventures need to get rolling.

In addition to meeting with local banks, don't forget to compare interest rates and fees with credit unions and internet banks. If you have an above-average credit score, you should definitely shop around for the best loan opportunities you can find.

According to the SBA, "When applying for a loan, you must prepare a written loan proposal. Make your best presentation in the initial loan proposal and application; you may not get a second opportunity. Always begin your proposal with a cover letter or executive summary. Clearly and briefly explain who you are, your business background, the nature of your business, the amount and purpose of your loan request, your requested terms of repayment, how the funds will benefit your business, and how you will repay the loan. Keep this cover page simple and direct. Many different loan proposal formats are possible. You may want to contact your commercial lender to determine which format is best for you. When writing your proposal, don't assume the reader is familiar with your industry or your individual business. Always include industry-specific details so your reader can understand how your particular business is run and what industry trends affect it." The SBA's website offers plenty of additional information about how to apply for a small business loan. Some of this information can be found at sba.gov/services/financialassistance/eligibility/applyLoan/index.html.

Government Loans (SBA Loans)

Depending on your background, you may be eligible for a government loan or government secured loan to help launch your business. For more information about SBA loans, visit sba.gov/services/financialassistance/sbaloantopics/index.html. If you're a military veteran, you may also be eligible for a special type of small business loan. According to the SBA, "The U.S. Small Business Administration has announced the SBA's Patriot Express Pilot Loan Initiative for veterans and members of the military community wanting to establish or expand small businesses." For additional information about loans for veterans, visit: sba.gov/patriotexpress/sba_patriot_expressloan.html.

Eligible military community members include:

➡ Veterans
➡ Service-disabled veterans
➡ Active-duty service members eligible for the military's Transition Assistance Program
➡ Reservists and National Guard members
➡ Current spouses of any of the above
➡ The widowed spouse of a service member or veteran who died during service or of a service-connected disability

Credit Cards

The biggest drawback to using your credit cards to fund your business startup is that most have high annual interest rates, often in the 20 to 30 percent range. This makes them a less attractive financing option, especially if you cannot pay off the balance for an extended period.

They are, nonetheless, still a funding option, especially if you have no others. If you are going to use your credit cards to fund your startup, try to pay off your balance(s) as quickly as possible. This will leave you carrying less debt, with lower monthly obligations, and with the opportunity to borrow more money if it's needed in the future.

Shop around for credit cards with the lowest interest rates and no annual fees. Many banks and credit unions offer small business credit cards (such as the Visa Small Business Card) that offer many special services—travel insurance and lower interest rates. You can shop for credit card deals from these websites: Bankrate.com, CardRatings.com, CreditCards.com, or LowerMyBills.com.

To properly analyze each credit card offer, determine the following information *before* completing an application:

- Whether there's an annual fee and how much it is.
- Is there an application or processing fee associated with completing the credit card application.
- What is the APR (annual percentage rate)? The lower the APR, the better. Some credit card offers have an Introductory APR, which only lasts for the first 3, 6, or 12 months. If this is the case, understand what the APR will revert to after this initial period.
- What is the default APR? If you're late on just one monthly payment, skip a payment for whatever reason, pay your monthly bill with a check that ultimately bounces, or don't adhere to the terms of the card holder agreement, your APR could automatically jump to the default rate, which is often well over 32.4 percent.
- What fees and charges are associated with the card? Most cards have late-fees, over-limit fees, balance transfer fees, online payment fees, telephone payment fees, and other hidden fees associated with them. These fees can add up quickly if you choose the wrong credit card or don't adhere to the terms of the cardholder's agreement.
- What perks or benefits are associated with the card?

Social Lending

This is a relatively new concept when it comes to borrowing money. Instead of turning to a traditional bank, credit union, or financial institution, using a social lending service, you can borrow money from everyday people looking for an interest-earning investment opportunity.

While having a better-than-average credit score is definitely beneficial, using this method for borrowing money allows you to tell your unique story to the potential lender(s) and take advantage of a more personalized approval process. The interest rates associated with this type of loan vary, based on your credit score.

Keep in mind, just because you're not borrowing through a traditional bank does not mean you can default on the loan without negative repercussions. If you're late on payments or default on a loan, the credit bureaus will be notified and a collections agency will be hired to recover the funds. For additional information about social lending, visit Prosper.com or Lending Club.com.

Investors

If you need $150,000 or more, it might make sense to seek out venture capital from one or more private investors (sometimes referred to as *angel investors*) or from an investment capital firm. A private investor can be found almost anywhere. It could be a friend, relative, or an entrepreneur looking for a viable investment opportunity. Typically, an investor will receive interest on her loan as well as a stake (equity) in the company. In a slow economy, finding investors is extremely challenging, especially if your unproven company is looking for large sums of money. It's often easier to seek out small amounts of investment capital from people you know and who will be passionate about your project and want to help you. No matter what method you use to find and raise investment capital, you'll first need to develop a well-written business plan that clearly describes your business idea and viability, plus gets the reader really excited about your business' potential.

According to Small Business Notes website (smallbusinessnotes.com/financing/angelinvestors.html), "Angel investors are individuals who invest in businesses looking for a higher return than they would see from more traditional investments. Many are successful entrepreneurs who want to help other entrepreneurs get their business off the ground. Usually they are the bridge from the self-funded stage of the business to the point that the business needs the level of funding that a venture capitalist would offer. Funding estimates vary, but usually range from $150,000 to $1.5 million."

An investment capital firm is more appropriate for companies capable of generating more than $25 million in revenue within five years. For a list of *Entrepreneur* magazine's Top 100 investment capital firms, visit entrepreneur.com/vc100/index.html.

Leasing and Renting

Leasing or renting equipment is another financing strategy that might not fund your entire business startup, but can greatly reduce the amount of hard cash you need to get things rolling. Renting equipment or tools means you do not take ownership in any form. You simply pay the rental rate for the time you need the equipment and return it when it's no longer needed. Leasing also means you do not own the equipment, but you are legally bound to pay for a portion of the entire value of the equipment, plus interest by way of scheduled monthly lease payments.

One benefit of renting or leasing equipment, such as computers, is you need little if any money upfront, which leaves you cash free to buy merchandise that can be resold for a profit right away. Also, rental and lease payments are deductions, unlike the sliding scale of tax depreciation used on owned equipment.

Supplier Terms

Another way to kick off your own business with minimal upfront costs is to ask your new suppliers for a revolving credit account, which gives you up to 90 days to pay for goods and services you need to operate your business or for resale to customers for a profit. People with strong credit will have few problems opening revolving credit accounts with suppliers. If your credit is not so strong, you will need to establish a payment history with most suppliers prior to their granting you credit privileges.

The advantage of revolving credit is that you can often sell your goods long before you have to pay your supplier. In effect, your suppliers are bankrolling your business and you get to skim off the profits, all without having to use your own cash.

Banking

Once your business is registered and ready to roll, you need to open a commercial bank account, separate from your personal savings or checking account. To do this, select the bank you want to work with, and then schedule an appointment to open an account. Be sure to shop around for a bank that offers the best and most convenient services, as well as the lowest fees. When you sit down with a banker, make sure you bring personal identification as well as your business name registration papers (incorporation papers) and business license because these documents are required to open a commercial bank account.

The next step is to deposit funds into your new account. If your credit is sound, this is also the time to ask the bank to attach a line of credit to your account, which can prove very useful if you need to borrow money down the road. Also, inquire about a credit card merchant account and other small business services that the bank offers.

Setting Up the Books

Money management can be tricky business because, in addition to customers/clients, cash flow is what keeps your business operational. Consequently, understanding money management should become a priority, even if you elect to hire an accountant or bookkeeper to manage your business' books. No matter what choice you make here, you still need to familiarize yourself with basic bookkeeping and money management principles. In addition, you'll need to understand how credit actually works as well as how to read bank statements and tax forms. It's also important that you understand the basic principles of accounts receivable and accounts payable.

When it comes time to set up your financial books, you have three options—do it yourself, hire an accountant or bookkeeper to do it, or a mix of both. You can do both by keeping your own books and hiring an accountant to prepare year-end financial statements and tax forms.

If you opt to keep your own books, make sure you invest in accounting software, such as Intuit's popular QuickBooks Pro software (877-683-3280/ quickbooks.com), because they are easy to use and make bookkeeping much easier than doing it manually.

Most accounting software also allows you to create client accounts with invoicing and mail merge options and to track account bank balances, merchant account information, and accounts payable and receivable. QuickBooks Pro, which is probably the most popular accounting software on the market for small businesses, is priced at $199.95 and is available wherever software is sold or directly from Intuit's website.

CLICK TIP

Be sure to track and record every cent coming in and going out of your business. Obtain receipts for everything you buy or spend money on for business.

Keep in mind that even with the proliferation of accounting software, hiring an accountant to take care of more complicated money matters is often wise. Like many professionals, accountants pride themselves on the fact that they do not cost you money, but rather make you money by discovering items overlooked on tax returns, by identifying business deductions you never knew existed, and by creating financial plans that enable you to enjoy the fruits of your labor later in life without having to worry about where the money will come from. If you are unsure about your bookkeeping abilities, even with the aid of accounting software, hire a bookkeeper to do your books on a monthly basis, and an accountant to audit the books quarterly and prepare year-end business statements and tax returns.

Remember to keep all business and tax records in a dry and secure place for up to seven years. This is the maximum amount of time the IRS and Revenue Canada can request past business revenue and expense information.

Purchase Payment Options

In today's super competitive business environment, consumers have come to expect many payment options for purchases. A steadfast, cash-only payment policy is no longer acceptable even for the small business operator, especially if you plan on doing business online. You must provide customers with multiple ways to pay, including cash, debit card, credit card, and electronic cash. There is a cost to provide these payment options—account fees, transaction fees, equipment rental, and merchant fees based on a percentage of the total sales value. But, these expenses must be viewed as a cost of doing business in the 21st century.

Be sure to shop around for the best service with the best prices. Not all banks, merchant accounts, and payment processing services are the same, and fees vary widely. Remember, consumers expect choices when it comes time to pay for purchases, and if you elect not to provide these choices, you can expect fewer sales.

Major Credit Card

In today's competitive business world, it's essential that as a business operator, you're able and willing to accept credit cards as payment for your products and/or services. Thus, you'll need to establish a *merchant account* with a bank, financial institution, or credit card merchant account provider, so you can accept Visa, MasterCard, American Express, and Discover.

Keep in mind, there are costs associated with accepting credit card payments which must be calculated into your cost of doing business (or passed along to your customers when you set your pricing).

It's important to shop around for the best deal when trying to acquire a merchant account, because fees vary dramatically. In addition to contacting local banks, do a search using Google or Yahoo! using the search phrase "Merchant Account."

Cash and Checks

The first way to get paid is by accepting cash, which is great because it is instant, with no processing time or fees required. As fast as the cash comes in, you can use it to buy more goods to sell and increase revenues and profits.

The major downside is that cash is risky because you could get robbed or lose it. In that instance, collecting from your insurance company could prove difficult if there is no paper transaction as proof. Even if you prefer not to receive cash, there are people who will pay in cash. For this reason, invest in a good-quality safe for your home and for use on the road. Also get in the habit of making daily bank deposits during daylight hours.

For a small business operator, accepting paper checks from people or companies you don't know is not a sound business strategy. It's too easy for people to write bad checks, which results in a loss of revenue as well as fees imposed by your bank. If you decide to accept a personal or business check from a customer, ask to see picture ID and write the customer's driver's license number on the back. If the amount of the check exceeds a few hundred dollars, ask the buyer to get the check certified or pay you using a bank draft or money order instead. The last thing you want to be left holding is a rubber check.

Debit Cards

Buying or renting a wireless or wired debit card terminal allows you to accept debit card payments, which is much better than accepting checks and in some ways better than cash—you do not have the theft concerns. When you acquire a merchant account to accept major credit cards, you will also be able to accept debit card payments from your customers.

Taxation and Your Business

There is no escaping the taxman, regardless of how big or small your business may be. If you earn business profits, the government will want its share. In the United States and Canada, business income/profits are taxed at the federal, state/provincial, and municipal levels. The best and most up-to-date information and advice you can obtain about small business and income tax will come directly from the Internal Revenue Service (800-829-3676, irs.gov) in the United States and the Canada Customs and Revenue Agency (800-959-2221, ccra-adrc.gc.ca) in Canada. These government agencies oversee federal business and income taxation.

Accountants can also help you navigate the murky taxation waters, and there are many books specifically developed to help the small business owner understand and prepare tax forms. Small-business taxation is complicated and can be very frustrating for the novice entrepreneur to understand. Even seasoned entrepreneurs do not like dealing with tax issues and preparing forms because the rules and regulations change regularly.

Paying Taxes

How your business is legally structured determines the taxes you pay, both personal and business, as well as the forms you're required to file. As a sole proprietor or unincorporated partnership, the income your business earns after expenses is your personal income, and you are taxed accordingly.

If your business is incorporated, you are taxed on the income you receive from the corporation in the form of wages and bonuses, and the corporation is taxed on the profits it earns after all expenses are deducted. Additionally, post-tax corporate profits are taxed once again when distributed to shareholders in the form of dividends.

Keep in mind that if you have any employees, you will need to obtain employee identification numbers, prepare and submit employee income tax reporting forms, and withhold and remit the employee and employer portions of Medicare, employment insurance, and Social Security.

There are a number of tax advantages from operating a homebased business. Because of allowable business expenses, it is very possible to claim a portion of your current household expenses, such as rent or mortgage payments and utility bills, against your business and personal income, especially for the sole proprietor. Whenever you are unsure about which expenses are allowable and which are not, it is best to contact an accountant.

The IRS provides small business owners with a number of free publications to explain small-business taxation issues. These publications can be used as a guide for completing small business and self-employment tax forms. You can pick up IRS small-business information, tax forms, and publications in person at your local IRS office, call to have the publications delivered by mail, (800) 829-3676, or download them online at irs.gov/business/small.

Your Workspace

Homebased workspace options range from any corner of a room, to an entire room, to a separate outside structure. Many people opt to use a converted garage, den, basement, or a spare bedroom as a business space. Each of these locations has advantages and disadvantages you'll want to consider before setting up shop.

Your first thought must be the daily living needs of your family and how space in the home is currently being utilized for day-to-day living as well as for special occasions, seasonal activities, and guests. Because setting up a home workspace requires balancing the needs of your business with the needs of your family, compromises will have to be made on both fronts.

If you plan to work from home, your workspace must be conducive to allowing you to work efficiently and provide ample space for you to conduct your business and possibly store your inventory. Make sure the space offers a suitable work environment from a noise, lighting, temperature, and layout standpoint. Is the office space wired for internet access, and does it possess enough electrical outlets? When working, will you be able to close the door and block out any family distractions, such as your kids at play or your dog barking?

Working out of two or three separate areas of the home is far less productive than working from one area. Will you constantly be searching for things rather than working? Try to make your workspace a single-use area. Ideally, the room should not double as the dining room at night or the children's playroom.

What tax implications are involved with operating a homebased business? You'll want to consult with an accountant before launching your business and later filing your annual state and federal income tax returns.

Welcoming Customers into Your Home

Working from home has many potential benefits, especially for a small business operator. If, however, your business will involve working with customers/clients in-person, and these people will be visiting your home office, workshop, or showroom, there are a variety of additional things to consider that relate to the functionality of your business, the professional image you hope to convey, and the ability of your home to easily and comfortably accommodate visitors. If you will be inviting clients or customers into your home, ask yourself the following questions:

- ➡ Are you legally able to welcome customers/clients into your home, based on local laws and ordinances?
- ➡ Do you have the interior/exterior space required to welcome customers/clients?
- ➡ Do you have suitable parking, and can you provide customers/clients with access to washroom facilities?
- ➡ Do you have ample space to separate your living space from your work/office space, to provide privacy for both customers and your family?

➡ Do you have a separate entrance for customers/clients?

➡ Is the appearance of your home conducive to welcoming people? (Peeling paint, threadbare carpets, and broken porch boards send customers and clients the wrong signals about your business and products. If your home needs a sprucing up, then do it before you get started.)

Storage Issues

Whether you have customers/clients coming into your home or not, you will need storage space for equipment, inventory, and business records, as well as adequate space for receiving products and shipping orders.

Provided you have enough storage space to meet your needs, the space you use will also need to be easily accessible, dry, and free of critters. It must also be secure, so there is no risk that valuable business equipment, inventory, and records will be stolen. If you do not have suitable storage space for inventory, is there suitable space for rent close by with good access? If so, how much will this increase your cost of doing business?

Equipment and Technology

Every business has different needs in terms of office furniture, equipment, and technology devices. If customers/clients will be visiting your homebased office, your furniture, equipment, and displays will need to reflect this, both in appearance and function. If you do not have people visiting your home office, you have more leeway because it won't really matter if the colors are mismatched, if you purchased your desk secondhand at your neighbor's garage sale, or if you built a few of the items yourself.

When it comes to your office furniture and equipment, all that really matters is that it's fully functional, reliable, and allows you to handle the day-to-day responsibility of your operation. Some of your office needs might include:

➡ *Desk and comfortable chair.* You will need a desk large enough for a computer monitor with tower storage underneath, a printer, and a telephone/fax machine. However, you can save space using a laptop computer, if necessary. Full-size Apple iMac desktop computers also tend to require less desk space. If you only splurge for one piece of office furniture, a comfortable and ergonomically correct office chair should be that luxury item, especially if your business keeps you in your seat for long periods of time. (Your back, neck, and shoulder will thank you!)

➡ *Paper file storage*. Even in this electronic age, businesses still generate lots of paperwork and paper-based files. You'll definitely need file cabinets to properly organize and store these files.

➡ *Worktable*. Purchase or build a worktable that is separate from your desk. Worktables are indispensable and can be used for opening and sorting mail, book- and record-keeping duties, packing and unpacking inventory, and much more. Just make sure you keep this work space clear and clutter free when it's not in use.

➡ *Computer system and software*. You will need a complete computer system, including monitor, printer, modem, keyboard, and mouse. The main considerations will be processing speed and data storage capabilities. You will also need software. Depending on the products and services you sell, you might need software in one or more of the following areas: word processing, accounting, database management, website building and maintenance, payment processing, inventory tracking, and desktop publishing. In general, Windows desktop computers cost less than laptop computers. Apple Mac computers tend to cost a bit more, but many people find them much easier to use, more ergonomic, and more space efficient.

➡ *Digital camera*. Digital cameras are often indispensable to online entrepreneurs. You can take pictures of products, and because the images (photographs) use digital technology, they are easily transferred to your website, e-mails, classified ads, or desktop publishing programs to create fliers, brochures, presentations, catalogs, posters, and signs. When it comes to choosing a digital camera, the higher the resolution (number of megapixels) the better. What's absolutely essential is that your product photographs look professional. This will probably mean you'll need to invest in backgrounds and specialized lighting equipment to create a mini photo studio. If you can't achieve the professional results you need by taking your own photos, either use stock photography provided by the manufacturers of the products you'll be selling or hire a professional photographer.

➡ *Telephone(s)/fax machine.* You will need a desktop telephone with business functions, such as on-hold, conferencing, redial, speakerphone, and message storage capabilities. You'll also need some type of answering machine or remote voice mail system. If your budget allows, you might consider purchasing an all-in-one office document center with a telephone, fax, printer, scanner, and copier. However, you'll still want a separate, full-feature telephone, perhaps equipped with a good-quality telephone headset, situated on your desk.

➡ *Cellular telephone.* A cellular telephone is a must, enabling you to keep in constant contact with customers, clients, and prospects, no matter where you are. Consider purchasing a Smartphone or Wireless PDA such as an Apple iPhone, BlackBerry, or Palm Treo that also has internet features, so you can receive, check, and send e-mails.

➡ *Internet connection.* Within your office, you will need a high-speed broadband, FIOS, or DSL internet connection so you can access the web. Depending on the layout of your office, the number of computers you'll be using, and where you'll need to connect to the internet, setting up wireless (Wi-Fi) internet access in your home or office may be beneficial. Depending on your service provider, a high-speed internet connection should cost between $30 and $60 per month.

➡ *Lighting.* Especially if your office doesn't have windows, you'll definitely want to install ample lighting. Avoid florescent lighting or any lighting that will cause eyestrain or fatigue. No matter when you're working (day or night), you want your office and workspace to be well lit.

Chapter 5

Online Income Opportunities

*O*nce you've decided to establish an online presence as an independent freelancer, whether your specialty involves website design, graphic design, or photography, there are a wide range of additional services, products, and downloadables you can offer through your website to generate revenue.

During the early stages of brainstorming ideas for your business and when you're developing your detailed business plan, consider not just the overall purpose and goals of your

CLICK TIP

A downloadable product can be a digital photograph, logo, website template, audio or video file, a font you've designed, or another form of digital artwork that you've created or own the copyright to that you plan to sell or license. The visitor to your website will be able to pay for and then download the item via your website. The process can be totally automated.

intended business, but also all of the ways you will ultimately generate revenues by offering services, products, and downloadables for a fee. As you make this determination, it dictates the functionality and features your website requires.

Say, for example, you're a website designer or graphic artist who wants to use your online presence as an online portfolio to showcase your best work and attract new clients. For this, the functionality required of your website is different than that required if you also opt to sell physical products that will need to be shipped to consumers (via an e-commerce module of your website) or choose to offer downloadable products that your consumers will pay for online and then download directly to their computer.

If you'll be doing custom work for your clients, such as website or graphic design, these services can be sold online. A potential customer would view your online portfolio, choose from a menu of services, pay for the desired

GENERATE ADDITIONAL REVENUE BY EXPANDING YOUR OFFERINGS

As you consider ideas for your online business, think about products and services you can offer that will benefit your customers, help to differentiate your business from the competition, and offer additional money-making opportunities. For example, if you're a website designer, in addition to offering your actual site design services, for an additional fee you can offer web page editing/updating services, search engine optimization services, and/or website hosting services to your clients. Tap your own creativity and take a close look at what products and services your competition is offering as you determine how you'll fully utilize your website as a profit-generating tool.

services online, and then expect to receive his custom-created work via e-mail or through an ftp site within a predetermined period. Many website designers and graphic artists are able to generate a significant amount of freelance work using their website, without ever directly interacting with clients in person or on the telephone.

This chapter focuses on just some of the ways an independent freelancer can generate revenues by fully utilizing their online presence while tapping their own unique skill set, interests, and specialties. Of course, once your online business is established, you can later expand it to add more revenue-generating opportunities.

The following is information about a dozen proven business models and ideas independent freelancers can utilize on their websites to generate additional revenue.

Website Design Services (Custom Work for Hire)

As a website designer/programmer, you should have the skills necessary to design, create, program, and publish websites on behalf of clients. This business model involves soliciting clients interested in hiring you on a freelance basis to handle their web design needs, which would involve your being paid either by the hour or on a per-project basis for your work. By offering web design services via your own website, you can invite prospective customers to view an online portfolio of your work, and then provide an online price list for your services, which can then be ordered and paid for online.

If you opt to interact with your clients entirely online, it's often easier to offer web design packages that include services that are clearly defined and listed. This might include a predetermined number of individual web pages and domain name registration for a flat fee. It might also involve the prospective client selecting a template that you've previously designed or own the copyright to. Then you customize it, as opposed to creating a website from scratch. Obviously, customizing a template requires a lot less interaction with clients than designing a site from scratch, which makes using this business model more conducive for those looking to accept clients from around the globe but wishing to have only minimal direct interaction with them.

As the web designer, you can design your own templates or become an affiliate for an online company that does nothing but license website templates. As an affiliate for one or more of these companies, you'd get paid when one of your clients licenses a template, and then you generate additional revenue by performing customization work. You can also offer other value-added services such as domain name registration, photo editing, and logo creation.

Some of the hundreds of website template companies that have established potentially lucrative affiliate or resale programs include:

- ➡ Dream Templates: dreamtemplate.com/affiliates.shtml
- ➡ Hyper Templates: hypertemplates.com/aff-signup.php
- ➡ Template Monster: templatemonster.com/register_aff.php
- ➡ Template World: templateworld.com/affiliates.html
- ➡ Website Templates: websitetemplates.com/affiliate-program.html

When using this business model, it's essential that your website clearly states what types of website design services you offer and describes the terms and conditions of your work. It's your responsibility to offer an online contract that clearly states prices, what's included, deadlines, and the like.

CLICK TIP

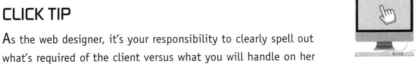

As the web designer, it's your responsibility to clearly spell out what's required of the client versus what you will handle on her behalf. For example, if you're setting up an e-commerce website for your client, you might make it her responsibility to provide the company logo (in digital form), all text to be incorporated into the site including the company background and product descriptions and the product photographs in a digital format. You might also make it her responsibility to register her own domain name and/or obtain her own credit card merchant account, and find her own ISP to host the site. However, these are additional services that you can handle on behalf of your clients and charge accordingly in order to offer a full-service operation and increase your income.

As the website designer, you can offer multiple pricing structures based on the work you're being hired to do. For example, you can charge one rate for customizing a website template, and a higher rate to do totally customized web design work (from scratch). You can also opt to charge a separate fee to update and/or maintain the website on your clients' behalf and offer additional a la carte services, based on your skills and the needs of your clients.

Keep in mind that if as a web designer you plan to offer custom website design services, which requires you to do the design work from scratch to meet your clients' unique needs, it will probably be necessary for you to communicate directly with him via e-mail, in person, or by telephone to review goals, needs, and expectations. Doing this type of work will be more time consuming than simply customizing a template with information and graphical assets provided by the client, so you can charge accordingly.

When companies or individuals hire a freelance website designer, their expectations will be high and they'll demand the following:

➡ Personalized attention and superior customer service/support
➡ Accurate price quotes
➡ Attention to detail
➡ Agreement between you and the client as to exactly what services will be provided
➡ Highly professional work
➡ Adherence to predetermined deadlines
➡ A finished product that meets their expectations and needs
➡ The willingness and ability on your part to address last-minute concerns, changes, and additions to the project
➡ Your availability when your client needs you for the current project or in the future
➡ Your willingness to create, sign, and adhere to a written contract

Only by meeting or exceeding the needs and expectations of your clients and offering your services at a fair and competitive price will you generate happy (repeat) customers and create the opportunity to generate positive word-of-mouth referrals, which for many freelancers represents the cornerstone of their business.

ALLOW YAHOO! AND eBAY TO REFER CLIENTS TO YOU

Companies that offer website turnkey solutions, including Yahoo! and eBay, have put together referral services to help potential website and online business operators find and hire freelancers to assist them in developing and launching their sites. For its Yahoo! Stores service, Yahoo! has compiled a list of "authorized partners" who are freelance website designers and graphic artists that the company refers to potential clients via a special web page (developernetwork.store.yahoo.com). For its ProStores service, eBay has also gathered a pool of freelance professionals called the Certified Designers Network that the company refers to its customers (prostoresdesign certification.com/servlet/StoreFront).

According to Yahoo!'s website, "The Yahoo! Merchant Solutions Developer Network is a group of professional web developers experienced at building e-commerce websites on the Yahoo! Merchant Solutions and Yahoo! Store platform. As part of this exclusive network, we offer this directory as a service to customers who may wish to hire a web expert to design their new site, upgrade their existing site, design advanced site templates, create specialized graphics, or handle complex technical requirements . . . If you qualify for inclusion in the directory, you will be listed free of charge. In the future we may offer fee-based services, such as sponsored listings with prominent placement. Inclusion and placement in this directory is at the sole discretion of Yahoo!. To be considered for inclusion in the Developer Directory, you must meet our Inclusion Guidelines. If you meet these guidelines, you are welcome to submit an application. Please be sure that you meet our guidelines before applying . . . . If you are approved for inclusion in the directory, your company name will appear within the Developer Directory. Merchants will be able to click your company name to access your full directory listing: company name, contact information, web address, company description, and link to your Yahoo!-based portfolio. To qualify for a portfolio link, you must have a portfolio page dedicated specifically to Yahoo! Store or Yahoo! Merchant Solutions websites."

According to eBay's website, "The ProStores Design Certification Program provides the training and resources you need to become proficient at designing and building

ALLOW YAHOO! AND eBAY TO REFER CLIENTS TO YOU, CONTINUED

stores on the ProStores platform. Get the benefit of marketing exposure with ProStores' rapidly growing merchant base and be authorized to display the credibility-building 'ProStores Certified Designer' logo." Training materials to become a ProStores Certified Developer are offered free of charge; however, there is a one-time $99 fee to take the certification exam that allows you to actually be certified.

Becoming a ProStores Certified Designer allows you, as a freelancer, to be listed in the ProStores Services & Software Directory, which will provide you with an ongoing source of new business leads and prequalified referrals. For freelance website designers and graphic artists, this program also pays referral fees if you help your own clients launch their e-commerce websites using the ProStores service. To learn more about the ProStores' affiliate program, visit prostores.com/estore_affiliate_program.html.

Both Yahoo! and eBay continue to spend millions of dollars annually to establish themselves as a leading e-commerce turnkey solution for anyone interested in launching an online business. With thousands of new customers joining these services every month, affiliation with either allows you to generate extra income and develop an ongoing flow of new business referrals that are prequalified and in need of your services. This is definitely a business model worth pursuing if you're looking to expand your client base and don't have a lot of time or money to invest in marketing your own services.

Website Design Downloadables
(Selling Templates and Predesigned Sites)

Instead of offering actual customized website design work, another website design business model involves creating website templates or complete predesigned websites and then selling them as downloadables via an e-commerce website. The customer then customizes his own template and publishes his own website using the downloadable products purchased from you.

This online business requires minimal interaction with clients beause the entire sales and purchase process is fully automated. After creating the templates and other downloadables you want to offer for sale, you simply design and launch an e-commerce website capable of selling and distributing downloadable goods. Once the site is launched, the majority of your time and resources will be spent promoting and marketing to drive traffic to the site.

The challenge to operating an online venture using this business model is that the downloadables you offer (i.e., the website templates), must be top quality, unique, easy to download and customize, and come with plenty of documentation for the customer. There are hundreds, perhaps thousands of online companies selling or licensing website templates. One way to differentiate yourself from the competition, and perhaps be able to charge a premium for your products, is to develop a specialty. This means creating specialized templates for specific types of websites, as opposed to more general purpose designs. Specialized websites and templates could be designed to meet the unique needs of companies working in specific fields or industries.

For example, you could create and sell website templates that are ideal for dentists, professional dog walkers, jewelers, or travel tour operators. The websites would offer the features and functionality people operating this type of business need. Using your template, they'd simply insert their company name, as well as their own text and photos, to create a fully customized website for themselves. If applicable, your template could include e-commerce (shopping cart) capabilities and other functionality required by an online business operator who wants to sell her own products online.

Simply selling website templates and other downloadables that you create is an easy online business to operate. The revenue potential, however, is lower than offering the actual website design and programming services. You simply can't charge as much to sell or license your templates and related downloadables.

Website Editing/Updating/Maintenance Services

Instead of offering website design work, a related business model involves charging an hourly rate to provide website editing and maintenance services to people who already have an established website but lack the knowledge to create new content, update their site, or properly maintain it. Offering this service requires some direct interaction with clients (via phone, e-mail, or in person), but far less than if you were to offer full website design services.

To succeed offering this type of service, you'll need to be proficient using a wide range of website development and editing tools, and have the knowledge required to quickly and efficiently edit an existing website that was designed and programmed by someone else. You must also be available to your clients when your services are needed and provide competitive pricing and quick turnaround.

Due to the high level of competition, it's best to charge a predetermined hourly rate for your services that's consistent with current market pricing but bill in 15-minute increments. To develop long-term customers, consider allowing people or companies you work with to prepurchase blocks of time at a discounted rate. For example, if you typically charge $50 per hour, allow clients to prepurchase a five-hour block of your time (with a one-year time period in which to utilize it) at a rate of $200.

Through your own website, you can not only promote this service and solicit new business but also offer a variety of other related services to generate additional revenue from the same clients, based on your skills and specialty, and the needs of your target customer base. If you have the skills, an additional service you could offer is personalized search engine optimization (SEO).

Search Engine Optimization Services

One of the most in-demand services from website operators and online business operators is for personalized search engine optimization (SEO) services. It's become essential to generate traffic from popular search engines because a website must have a prominently placed listing. Thus, individuals and companies are often willing to pay top dollar for a guarantee that their site will not just get listed with the search engines but will receive top placement.

Becoming a skilled SEO specialist requires that you stay up to date with the latest search engine listing procedures and that you become familiar with the various methods available for securing good listing placement. This involves incorporating keywords into website text, the use of meta tags, and the submission of carefully worded listings to the popular search engines.

In most cases, SEO services are an ongoing need among website operators. Thus, you can offer your services for an ongoing monthly fee based on how much time and effort you invest working for each client. This is a highly competitive business, but many of the companies and individuals who offer SEO services don't generate the desired results or charge extremely high prices for the most basic of services. It's essential that you develop a reputation for offering your clients positive results for a competitive price.

Be sure to study your competition carefully to determine what services are offered as well as pricing. Once you develop the skills and expertise needed to offer this type of service, you'll be able to use your website to generate business and take on new clients with minimal direct interaction with them.

A company offering comprehensive search engine optimization services will include:

➡ Personalized consultation with the website operator
➡ Keyword research specific to each web page or website
➡ Competitive analysis to help a client's website stand out from the competition in terms of relevance and search engine listings
➡ Copywriting or editing services for the client's website to properly incorporate keywords
➡ Website development/programming to create and add meta tags and other necessary elements to ensure prominent search engine listings
➡ Manual submission to the major search engines and automated submission to less popular search engines
➡ Regular reporting of search engine listings and placement/rankings
➡ Ongoing efforts to fine-tune and optimize SEO results

In addition to offering effective SEO solutions, you can also specialize in helping your customers/clients create, launch, and manage effective keyword advertising campaigns using services like Google AdWords or Yahoo! Search Engine Marketing. Many website operators rely on SEO and search engine marketing/advertising as a primary way to generate traffic to their sites. To succeed in offering this service in a competitive marketplace, you'll need to become highly proficient and knowledgeable using Google AdWords and related services, and develop an expertise in creating ads that generate better-than-average results for your clients.

There are a variety of online and in-person training programs that are designed to help you develop the necessary knowledge and skills to become an SEO and search engine marketing expert. Some of these training programs are available from:

➡ High Rankings: highrankings.com/home

➡ Search Engine College: searchenginecollege.com

➡ Search Engine Guide: searchengineguide.com

➡ Search Engine Strategies: searchenginestrategies.com

➡ Search Engine Workshops: searchengineworkshops.com/registration.html

➡ Search Marketing Expo: searchmarketingexpo.com

➡ SeoBook: seobook.com/join/

➡ World Wide Learn: worldwidelearn.com/online-training/search-engine-positioning.htm

---

CLICK TIP

To learn more about the search engine marketing programs offered by Google, Yahoo! and Microsoft, visit their websites: Google AdWords (adwords.google.com/select/CampaignSummary), Yahoo! Small Business Search Engine Marketing (sem.smallbusiness.yahoo.com/searchenginemarketing/), and Microsoft AdCenter (adcenter.microsoft.com/).

Web Browser Compatibility Testing

There are several different web browsers used by surfers around the world. While Microsoft's Internet Explorer is certainly the most popular, other browsers like Firefox, Opera, and Safari (Apple's default browser for the Mac) are also commonly used. In addition to the different browsers, there are also multiple versions of each browser still in use, and some web surfers continue to use obsolete browsers like Netscape Navigator to surf the web.

With so many different browsers, browser versions, and optional browser plug-ins in use by people operating computers with different operating systems, compatibility issues are a growing concern among website operators who want to ensure that their site works flawlessly and provides the same visitor experience, regardless of what browser is being used. Website operators need quality browser compatibility testing to ensure their site works with all past and current web browsers, plug-ins, and related technologies. This is a service that freelance web designers can offer to customers/clients as a one-time value-added service or as a monthly, bi-monthly, semi-annual, or annual "check-up" service.

In addition to using a wide range of browsers and browser versions to visit a client's website to perform compatibility testing, there are also software and online-based tools you can use. Web browser compatibility testing tools and services include:

- ➡ Browser Cam: browsercam.com
- ➡ Browser Camp: browsrcamp.com
- ➡ Cross Browser Testing: crossbrowsertesting.com
- ➡ IE NetRenderer: ipinfo.info/netrenderer/
- ➡ SwatLab: swatlab.com/qa_testing/compatibility.html

Website Hosting Services

Designing and programming websites is one need you can provide as a website designer; however, many individuals and small- to medium-size companies also require independent website hosting services. You can purchase and maintain the necessary equipment to provide your own website hosting services in-house. You can also take a more cost-effective approach and develop a partnership or alliance with a well-established ISP or website hosting company that will offer you on ongoing commission for referring your clients to them. An even simpler option is to sign up as an affiliate for one or more established website hosting companies and simply offer your clients/customers a link from your website to a hosting service's website in exchange for a flat per-click fee or ongoing commission.

Some website hosting companies also offer resale programs to website developers/programmers. That provides a more lucrative and flexible revenue-generating solution and allows you, the website designer, to bundle website hosting services with your other services without the client having to go elsewhere. For a low, flat monthly fee, many of these web hosting services allow you to host an unlimited number of websites on their servers.

Just a few examples of website hosting companies that offer reselling opportunities to freelance website designers are:

➡ Dundee Internet Services: dundee.net/isp/whole.htm
➡ eHost Pros: ehostpros.com/reseller/reseller.html
➡ EZ web Hosting: ez-web-hosting.com/reseller.htm
➡ Host Gator: hostgator.com/resellers.shtml
➡ iPower Web: ipowerweb.com/reseller/index.html
➡ Lightning Services: lightningservers.net
➡ Site5: site5.com/resellers/
➡ The Planet: theplanet.com/resellers/default.asp

Using any search engine, enter the phrase "Reseller web hosting" to find additional providers.

Graphic Arts (Custom Work for Hire)

Just as web designers can utilize their website to promote themselves and generate work from new clients located anywhere in the world, this process is even easier for freelance graphic artists, who can offer specific services such as letterhead, business card, or company logo design services for sale via their website.

If you want to develop and promote yourself as a logo design specialist, develop your website so it offers several pricing plans for packages, such as five to ten custom logo design variations for a pre-set price. You can also offer similar services for business card or company letterhead design, newsletter layout, or any other graphic design-related services that can be promoted and ordered via a website.

To succeed offering this type of service, you'll need to be proficient using a wide range of graphic design tools. You must also be available to your clients and provide competitive pricing and quick turnaround.

CLICK TIP

Using your website to promote your graphic design services, consider promoting a menu of available services that you offer. For example, you might offer logo design, photo retouching/editing, custom illustrations, newsletter/publication design, business card design, company letterhead design, or other services that you decide to specialize in. To help differentiate yourself in the marketplace, consider focusing on a specialty or targeting your services to a specific and unique market/customer base.

For professional photographers, one company that offers a complete online turnkey solution that's affordable, yet very flexible in terms of the functionality offered, is Pictage (310-525-1552/pictage.com). In addition to allowing photographers to create their own e-commerce website, Pictage also serves as a full-service photo printing lab.

If you plan to offer custom graphic design services, which require you to do the design work from scratch to meet each client's unique needs, it will probably be necessary for you to communicate directly with them either via e-mail, in person, or by telephone to review their goals, needs, and expectations.

USE THE WEB TO FIND FREELANCE JOBS

As a freelance web professional, one way to find and generate new business via the web is to utilize a service such as Guru.com or eLance.com that helps to match qualified freelancers with businesses in need of their services. Chapter 14 focuses on how to best utilize these services as a freelancer and features an exclusive interview with Inder Guglani, the CEO of Guru.com, who provides additional tips for freelancers on how to use the web to generate business and additional income. In addition to responding to work-for-hire ads from companies who need freelancers, these services can help you create an online portfolio of your work that can be used in addition to or instead of your own website to market yourself and your services.

Graphic Arts Downloadables
(Selling Digital Artwork, Fonts, Logos, and Photos)

As a graphic artist, you might opt to create your own artwork or other saleable products and offer your creations for sale on the web. The products you sell might include website templates you've created, unique fonts or typestyles, themed clip art, other types of downloadables, or digital artwork (including photographs, drawings, or illustrations) that can be printed out, framed, and sold via an e-commerce website. What you offer will determine your target audience and how your products should be marketed and distributed.

Custom Photography Services

There are many specialties a photographer can pursue, such as portrait work, weddings or special events photography, commercial photography, or pet photography. Regardless of your specialty, your website can be used to promote and showcase your work, and allow prospective clients to book appointments and pay a deposit for a sitting fee, for example. Your website can also be used to sell prints and other photo products from custom shoots directly to customers through an e-commerce turnkey site (designed specifically for photographers) that requires minimal interaction on your part.

> **CLICK TIP**
>
>
> SmugMug (smug mug.com) offers complete website turnkey solutions for photographers that require no programming. Visit JasonRich Photography.com to see a working sample site for a photographer.

If you offer custom photography services of any kind, the priority of your website should be to showcase your very best work and to separate yourself from your competition in terms of work quality and professionalism. As a photographer, you can charge premium pricing for top-quality work that meets the customer's needs.

Stock Photography Sales and Licensing (Downloads)

Many photographers develop vast collections of stock photography that they license or sell online via their own website. This is yet another business model available to photographers, and one that requires very little direct interaction with customers once you set up an e-commerce website capable of selling/licensing your images and processing online payments.

Photo Editing/Retouching Services

For photographers who are proficient using PhotoShop CS3 (CS4), Apple Aperture 2, or another professional-quality digital photo editing software package, you can offer photo editing and retouching services via your website. This can include working on custom images you shoot for your client or editing/retouching images that the client supplies to you via e-mail.

Many freelance photographers charge a separate (hourly or flat) fee for photo editing/retouching that's above and beyond what they charge for actual photo shoots and/or prints.

Photo Product Sales

Many photo labs that cater to professional photographers now offer the ability to resell a wide range of photo-related products such as T-shirts, mugs, greeting cards, photo books, mouse pads, puzzles, and dozens of other products created from photographs. This, of course, is in addition to offering prints in a wide range of sizes and finishes.

Companies like CaféPress (cafepress.com) offer photo-related products. However, services like SmugMug that cater to professional photographers

CLICK TIP

One rather unique product that professional photographers can offer to clients as a reseller via their own website is Fotoflots® (fotoflot.com/index.html). These are photographs that are professionally printed on Fuji Crystal Archive paper and then mounted onto 1/8-inch acrylic. It's a unique product that's available in many different sizes and offers a contemporary-looking alternative to framing any color or black-and-white photograph.

also offer photo products that can be marked up, so photographers can sell the products via their own websites and earn a generous markup.

Extra revenue can also be earned by custom framing prints or selling custom photo canvases, creating and selling photo books and albums, or by selling your prints in other formats. These products can all be sold directly to customers via your website or by establishing an affiliate relationship with companies like CaféPress.

Reselling Turnkey Solutions

In addition to services that sell website templates, there are many companies that offer complete turnkey solutions for people to design, publish, and manage their own website or online business. One way you can increase your online revenues as a web designer or graphic artist is to become a reseller or affiliate for any of these website turnkey solution providers. You earn commissions by reselling the various products or by referring your customers/clients to these turnkey solution providers.

eBay's ProStores service offers a complete turnkey solution for anyone interested in designing, launching, and managing a full-service e-commerce website, with absolutely no programming required. Like many companies that offer similar services, eBay has an established affiliate program (prostores .com/estore_affiliate_program.html) that allows website designers and other freelancers to earn commissions by referring business.

Yahoo! Small Business also offers a complete turnkey solution to anyone interested in designing, publishing, and managing a full-service e-commerce business. To learn more about Yahoo!'s affiliate program (of interest to website designers and other freelancers), visit smallbusiness.yahoo.com/webhosting /affiliate.php.

GoDaddy.com offers a competitive reseller plan (godaddy.com/gdshop /wwd_landing.asp) that allows freelance website designers, graphic artists, and others to resell the company's most popular website hosting, domain name registration, and other web-related services. GoDaddy.com is known for offering extremely competitive pricing, top-notch customer service, and a broad range of services of interest to anyone who wants to create or publish

> ## CLICK TIP
>
> **A**s a reseller, another service you can offer to your customers/clients via your website is the ability to sign up for and manage a credit card merchant account. These accounts allow them to accept credit card payments via their own websites. To find companies that have competitive reseller programs for merchant accounts, enter the search phrase "reseller credit card merchant account" into Google or another popular search engine.

any type of website. As a reseller, you can earn money (in the form of commissions) by offering GoDaddy's services to your clientele. The company also offers an affiliate program.

Generate Multiple Revenue Streams from Your Website

The best way to generate the most revenue possible via your online presence as a web designer, graphic artist, or photographer is to offer several different types of services as well as value-added services or products to your customers/clients. This chapter offered just a few suggestions for the types of services and/or products you could offer and the type of business model you could utilize.

By becoming a reseller for multiple types of services, you can earn extra money from commissions and referrals through your website while at the same time focusing on offering the types of professional services you specialize in. In most cases, becoming a reseller for another company, whether it's to sell website templates, a website creation turnkey solution, or photographic services, for example, costs you little or no money upfront. What's required is that you effectively market the service on your website to your customers and clients.

Before signing up to become a reseller or affiliate with any company, do some research to ensure the company is reputable, offers top-quality and reliable services, and offers not just competitive retail pricing but competitive commissions (which is how you'll earn your money). Think twice before paying to become an affiliate or reseller, unless you'll receive something of value for the fees you initially pay to set up your account with the company. For every company that charges freelancers to become resellers or affiliates, for example, you should be able to find at least a dozen additional companies that offer similar services without charging a fee.

Chapter 6

Online in One Week or Less

*D*epending on your goals, you may be planning to conduct most or all of your business via the web by selling products and/or offering your services as a web designer, graphic artist, or photographer directly to customers and clients throughout the world. In this situation, your website will probably require an e-commerce component so you can take and process orders via the web, as well as accept online payments.

As you'll discover from this chapter, however, this will be only one of the components your website will need in order to be a valuable business tool. Even if you plan to conduct the majority of your business locally and in person (working directly with your clients), having a professional-looking website can be a powerful promotional, sales, and marketing tool for yourself and your business by allowing you to showcase your portfolio of work. The planning, design, and launching your business' online presence is a process that can be done in one week once you have all of the content needed for the website and a completed portfolio of work to showcase.

As a website designer, creating a website from scratch that truly showcases your ability to create an original and highly functional site is essential. However, as a graphic designer or photographer, where showcasing and selling your work/service is more essential than the originality of the website itself, using a website turnkey solution helps you get online faster, easier, and without programming.

The Purpose of Your Website

Before you can create and launch a website from which to operate your business, carefully and clearly define the purpose of your online presence. During this early planning phase, answer the following questions:

→ What are you trying to accomplish with your website? For example, will you be selling your services online and allowing people to hire you via the web? Or, will you be selling products or downloadable content? Perhaps you'll simply use your online presence as a promotional tool to showcase your portfolio of work. Chapter 5 outlined some of the ways website designers, graphic artists, and photographers can generate revenue from a website. Now, you must determine how you'll actually be utilizing your online presence.

→ Who is the website targeted to?

→ What information and content is included on the site?

→ What functionality is required from the website to accomplish your objectives?

→ How will you drive traffic to your website?

Much of the functionality and required content for your website is determined by the goals you set for yourself and your overall objectives. This should all be outlined in your written business plan.

The Best Design Approach

Once you know exactly what you're trying to accomplish, who your target audience is, and what functionality is important to you, you can begin focusing on the very best ways to communicate your core messages to your intended online audience. Through your website, you can use text, graphics, photographs, animations, audio, video, and other multimedia content to promote yourself and your work. These same communication tools can also be used to market and sell your products/services.

However, just because you have the ability to use interactive multimedia elements (including animations, video, and streaming audio, for example) as part of your website, doing so might not be conducive to communicating your overall message and for achieving your desired results. At this point, you'll want to tap your own creativity to determine how you can use the many tools and resources available to you to create your unique online presence.

Throughout the website design and planning phase, strive to incorporate the content and functionality you deem appropriate. Also remember to directly address the wants and needs of your target audience. Create a website that is:

➡ *Easy to navigate*. Within moments of accessing your website, visitors should be able to find the information or content they're looking for. The user interface, menus, and overall layout should all be intuitive. If visitors have to spend more than a few seconds searching for what they're looking for or can't immediately obtain the answers to their questions, they'll simply surf to another website.

➡ *Welcoming*. Again, within moments of accessing your website, visitors should discover that their wants and needs can and will be met by what's offered. The visitor should feel welcome and quickly develop confidence in your site.

➡ *Professional looking*. These days anyone can design and publish a website in a few hours. Your website, however, must look professional and be somewhat unique. It should help you convey your positive reputation, showcase your accomplishments, build up a potential customer/client's confidence, and quickly communicate your key message(s). What you say is important, but equally important is the way you utilize colors, fonts, text, graphics, photos, and other elements to create a visually pleasing site.

➡ *Error-free.* One of the biggest mistakes you can make when creating a website that's designed to promote you and your business or sell products/services directly to customers/clients is to publish a website that contains errors. Spelling or grammatical mistakes, misleading or incorrect information, or dead links are common errors that will reduce your credibility and detract from the professional image you're trying to convey.

Cater to Your Target Audience

Whether you plan to operate an e-commerce business or use your online presence for promotion, you want to define very specific objectives for your website and then develop content that allows you to meet those objectives. At the same time, absolutely every aspect of your website should be designed and produced around the wants and needs of your target audience, your potential customers or clients.

Every menu option, feature, function, or piece of content added to your website should somehow cater to your target audience's wants and needs. During your website design stage, put yourself in the shoes of your target audience and think the way they think. Focus on their concerns, desires, objectives, challenges, and problems. Everything you offer on your website should somehow focus on solving their problems, offering them a solution to a situation they're facing, saving them money, maximizing their time, better utilizing their resources, enhancing their productivity, or addressing their other wants or needs. Your ability to anticipate and then address the wants and needs of your visitors while at the same time focus on your own goals and objectives means the difference between the success and failure of your online business venture.

Creating Your Own Website

Unless you're a website designer specifically trying to sell your own website designs skills, your ability to create and launch your online presence will be faster, easier, and less expensive if you take advantage of a complete website turnkey solution. Instead of having to hire a team of programmers to design and launch a website from scratch, which could take weeks or months to create and cost you thousands, if not tens of thousands, of dollars in development costs, a turnkey solution provides you with a selection of professional-looking website templates that you can customize with your own content (text, graphics, photos, animations, multimedia content).

Each template includes all of the components needed to create a highly functional website, including in many cases the ability to handle secure e-commerce transactions. Website hosting services and the ability to accept major credit cards and other online payment options is available for an additional fee, so you may not even need to acquire a separate merchant account. Many of the companies that offer turnkey solutions have even created an entire suite of easy-to-use, online tools to assist you in setting up and managing your online business.

While the many different website templates available to you may not offer flashy features you might like to incorporate into your site, they do offer the core functionality necessary to launch your online business and test its viability. Once your business is successful, you should definitely plan on expanding and fine-tuning your website on an ongoing basis.

The biggest benefits of using a turnkey solution to design, launch, and manage your website are:

- Low startup cost.
- A single company provides the development tools for the website itself and secure website hosting services. For an additional fee, the same company will facilitate the ability to accept multiple forms of online payments, including major credit cards, electronic checks, Google Checkout, and/or PayPal's Express Checkout.
- Absolutely no programming required.
- You can typically design and launch a basic site in less than a week.

➡ The ability to choose from dozens or even hundreds of professional-looking website templates, and then customize your favorite to give your site a unique look.

➡ Using the same suite of online tools, you can design, publish, maintain, and promote your site, and track traffic to the site and synchronize sales data to financial software applications such as Intuit Software's QuickBooks to better handle your record keeping and accounting. Many of the turnkey solutions also offer modules for maintaining a customer database, managing inventory, and keeping detailed order shipment records, with the ability to print shipping labels and track packages shipped via the U.S. Postal Service, FedEx, or UPS.

➡ Website templates are available for very specific business purposes. Thus, if you're a professional wedding photographer, there are templates that will allow you to promote yourself, showcase your work, and better service your customers by allowing them to order prints or wedding albums online. Specialized templates are available to handle a wide range of needs for graphic designers and photographers.

Before you start creating your website, whether it's from scratch or by customizing a template, spend time surfing the web looking for other sites that you consider to be top-quality and well-designed, and that you'd like to emulate. Determine in advance what features and functionality you want as well as what design elements you'd like to incorporate into your site. Knowing your immediate needs and what your needs might be in the future helps you choose a turnkey solution that's best suited to your business venture.

Every online business has different needs based on what's being sold, to whom the products/services are being sold, and what features and functionality need to be incorporated into the site. Once you pinpoint what you want and need, finding a complete turnkey solution that meets your requirements at a price you can afford is relatively straightforward.

As you look at what each turnkey solution offers, don't just look at a list of features and make your decision. Visit several websites that currently use the services of the company you're thinking about working with, and invest time exploring those websites. Your own site will be customized, of course, but do the sites you're looking at offer the professional look, functionality, and user interface that could work well for your business model and image? Will you be able to easily customize the templates to create a site you're proud of and meets your needs?

Ultimately, choosing the best turnkey solution could mean the difference between success and failure. In addition to comparing the startup costs and ongoing monthly fees associated with each of these services, some of the things you'll also want to evaluate before choosing a specific solution include:

- ➡ The tools and resources offered by the service provider.
- ➡ The quality and selection of the site templates being offered.
- ➡ The ease of use of the design tools and other resources offered to help operate your business.
- ➡ The technical support services provided by the solution provider.
- ➡ The functions that can be easily incorporated into your website using the development tools provided.
- ➡ The ability to accept and process online payments from customers/clients.
- ➡ The online security measures your site can incorporate.
- ➡ Resources offered to help you market and promote your online presence.
- ➡ The ability to easily integrate your site's order and customer data with your accounting, spreadsheet, and/or order management software.
- ➡ The ease of use, functionality, and professional appearance of the shopping cart module that will be incorporated into your site, if applicable, using the turnkey solution you select.
- ➡ The extra fees or charges you'll be responsible for in order to get your website designed, launched, and operational.
- ➡ The expandability of your site in the future, using compatible third-party tools and resources.

Domain Name

You can't have an online business without an address. So, after selecting the name of your business, you need to register your website's address (URL). This process takes just a few minutes and costs under $10 per URL if you use an internet registrar, such as GoDaddy.com (godaddy.com). The hard part is selecting an address that works.

Brainstorm the perfect website address for your company. Ideally, the address you select should be easy to remember, easy to spell, and obvious to potential web surfers. For example, if the name of your company is "ABC International," you might want your website address to be "ABC International.com." Obviously, with so many websites already in existence, many website domain names (URLs) are already taken. However, with more than 31.7 trillion URLs ending with the ".com" extension possible, there are still plenty of appealing domain names available.

A typical URL has three main components. The first part typically begins with "www." or "http://" The second part is what you must select. The third part is its extension, which is typically ".com." However, a variety of other extensions such as .edu, .org, .net., gov, .info, .TV, .biz, .name and .us are available. Some of these extensions have specific uses. For example, a website that ends with the extension ".gov" is a government-operated website. Most web surfers are accustomed to URLs ending with the popular ".com" extension— ideally, you want your URL to use it. Otherwise, potential customers might get confused trying to find your website if it utilizes a less popular extension.

Of course, the same website can have many different URLs that lead to the same place. So, you could potentially register www.abcinternational.com, www.abcinternational.biz, and www.abcinternational.info, to ensure web surfers are able to find you.

As you brainstorm the perfect URL, the part of the website address you customize can only use letters, numbers, and the hyphen symbol (-). No other special characters or punctuation marks such as !, #, $, or "," can be used. Also, no spaces can be used within a URL. You *can* use an underscore (_) to represent a space, but spaces can be confusing to web surfers, so it's not advisable.

The customizable part of a domain name combined with an extension such as .com can be up to 63 characters long. As a general rule, the shorter the domain name, the easier it is to remember and type into a web browser accurately. The very short names, of course, are gone. Virtually all of the one-, two-, three-, and four-character domain names have long since been taken. The customizable part of the domain name you select must be totally unique and not already registered by another person or company. It also may not violate someone else's copyrighted name, company name, or product name.

Domain names are not case sensitive, so you can mix and match upper- and lower-case letters to make a domain name easier to read and promote. For example, you could promote your domain name as "abccompany.com" or "ABCCompany.com" or "AbcCompany.com."

As you're in the process of brainstorming the perfect domain name for your business, come up with at least five to ten options you like. When you're ready to register your domain name, you first need to determine if the name you've selected is registered to someone else. This process takes under one minute.

Checking a Domain Name

To see if a domain name is registered to someone else, simply go to the website of any domain name registrar—GoDaddy.com, Register.com, Network Solutions.com, or MyDomain.com—and enter your desired domain name in the field marked "Start a domain search" or "Find a domain name." If the domain name you've entered is available, you will have the opportunity to register it on the spot for an annual fee.

You need to register your new domain name with an internet domain name registrar. There is an annual fee to register a domain name. Depending on the registrar, a single name costs $5.95 to $39.95 per year. Obviously, choose a company with the lowest rates. GoDaddy.com (godaddy.com) tends to offer very competitive rates for domain name registrations, and the process is extremely fast and easy.

Registering a Domain Name

Registering your domain name requires you to provide details about yourself and your company, including your name, address, phone number, and credit card information (for paying the annual fee). The process varies based on which domain registrar you use, but it should take no more than five to ten minutes to complete. After you've set up an account, registering additional domain names is much faster.

Part of the domain name registration process will probably involve providing the registrar with your internet service provider's IP address. You may also need to provide what are called DNS numbers to the registrar. This is information that will be provided by your internet service provider (ISP), if applicable. The ISP is the company that will be hosting your website. In this case, it'll probably be the company you select to provide you with an e-commerce turnkey solution.

Ideally, you want your website to have a single domain name that you can promote and can be remembered easily. But because some people have trouble spelling or get easily confused, you might want to register multiple domain names with slightly different spellings. This way, if someone accidentally types the wrong domain name into his web browser, he'll still wind up at your website. Think about some of the common typos or ways someone might misspell your domain name, and register those names as well.

Preparing Website Assets and Resources You'll Need

OK, you're just about at the point where you're ready to start putting together a website in order to go online. Because you're probably using an turnkey solution initially for your website, you won't be doing any programming. You simply choose a template and begin customizing it. To fully customize your site, there are some important design elements, referred to as *assets*, and website components that you want to create or have created on your behalf. They should be gathered or created before you start designing and putting your site together.

WARNING

Beware of copyright and trademark infringement! Make sure you have written permission to use any text, photos, graphics, illustrations, or other copyrighted or trademarked materials you plan to feature on your website. This applies to any material that you did not create from scratch and that you do not own the rights to. If you'll be using product artwork or product descriptions created by the manufacturer of the product(s) you're selling, for example, make sure you have permission to use them before incorporating them into your website.

For ease of implementation, acquire all of your assets in a digital format. For example, all photos, graphics, and illustrations should be available in a .JPG or .TIF graphic format. The following are original assets you'll probably want to create (or have created) for incorporation into your website:

➡ *Company logo.* You might consider hiring a professional graphic designer to create a professional-looking logo for your company if this type of work isn't your specialty.

➡ *Detailed and professionally written descriptions of your products/services.* These descriptions should contain no spelling or grammatical errors, be easy to read and understand, and provide potential customers with all of the information they'll want or need to know about your products/services.

➡ *Website text.* In addition to detailed product/service descriptions, a well-designed and professional website will have other text elements to educate the customer and convey your marketing message. For preplanning purposes, additional text elements you might want to add are:

· Company description and background information ("About Us")
· Press releases
· FAQ ("frequently asked questions") documents
· Shipping information
· Product return information
· Customer satisfaction guarantee and customer testimonials
· Contact information
· Website copyright information

➡ *Professional quality photos.* Because people shopping online won't be able touch and feel your product before they make a purchase, it's essential to provide the best quality photographs possible. These photos should not only show off your products in the best way possible, they should also showcase details about the product and allow web surfers to see the product from different vantage points.

➡ *Multimedia elements.* If you plan to incorporate animations, audio, or video into your website, you want to created them in advance. Adding flashy features to your site can be a useful marketing tool as long as what you've added doesn't become distracting or take away from your overall marketing or sales message.

➡ *Online portfolio of your work.* This is a place to showcase the work you've done to impress potential new customers/clients. More information about creating a portfolio can be found in Chapter 9.

Your Site Text

If you have a flare for writing and believe you can write copy for your site that will capture the attention of your visitors, effectively communicate your marketing message, and help sell your products/services online, then by all means you should write your own copy. It's essential, however, that in addition to being well-written, informative, and compelling your text must be error free in terms of spelling, punctuation, and grammar.

Because your customers will rely on the text elements on your website, such as your product/service descriptions, to make their buying decisions, seriously consider hiring a professional freelance writer or marketing expert to create these elements on your behalf. A freelance writer, advertising specialist, public relations professional, or marketing expert has the skills and experience to create well-written copy for your site.

You can find freelance writers using services, such as Guru.com or eLance.com. They are ideal for tracking down any type of experienced freelancer, whether it's a photographer, writer, editor, graphic designer, or website programmer. Plan on spending at least several hundred dollars to have a professional writer create product/service descriptions and other text elements such as your biography. An experienced writer typically charges between $.50 and $1 per word. Some charge a flat fee for a specific project. Avoid negotiating an hourly rate.

Professional Quality Photos

How well you depict your product(s) online, in terms of the quality of photographs you incorporate into your site, plays a tremendous role in building up your credibility and generating sales. After all, that timeless saying "A picture is worth a thousand words" definitely holds true. While your product descriptions are important, it's essential that you showcase your products visually whenever possible, using multiple, crystal clear, detailed, and full-color photographs.

If you're on a tight budget, consider contacting your product's manufacturer or distributor to determine if it has already created a selection of product images you can incorporate into your site. Another alternative is to contact a few stock photo agencies to see if you can acquire inexpensive, royalty-free images. To use these images, you either pay a fee per image or a flat fee to be able to use an unlimited number of images from the stock photo agency's library of images. A typical stock photo agency has a library consisting of hundreds of thousands or even millions of digital images you can download and use instantly. The following are a few stock photo agencies worth contacting to obtain stock photographs for your website:

- ➡ Microsoft: office.microsoft.com/en-us/clipart/default.aspx
- ➡ Adobe: adobe.com/products/creativesuite/stockphotos/
- ➡ Big Stock: bigstockphoto.com
- ➡ Comstock: Comstock.com
- ➡ FotoSearch: FototSearch.com
- ➡ iStock: iStockPhoto.com
- ➡ Shutterstock: Shutterstock.com

Another option is to take your own images using a high-resolution digital camera in a photo studio you set up in your home or office. If the product(s) you'll be photographing are small, you can set up an inexpensive desktop photo studio for a few hundred dollars (plus the price of a camera). For products that are larger, you'll need to use professional-quality lighting and backgrounds to create the images you need.

CLICK TIP

As a general rule, when taking product photographs, you want to use a solid color background. Depending on the product and how the photos will be used on your site, a solid white background typically works best. However, using photo editing software such as PhotoShop CS3 (CS4), you can crop away the background altogether, if desired.

For several hundred dollars, you can purchase the lighting and backgrounds needed to take professional shots. Lighting and background packages can be purchased from companies like Photography Lighting Company (photography-lighting.com) and Amvona (amvona.com). eBay.com is also a great place to find used or close-out professional photography equipment at discounted prices.

Once you've taken your product photos, you can edit and manipulate them as needed using software such as Adobe Photoshop Elements, Adobe Photoshop CS3 (CS4), Apple's iPhoto, or Apple's Aperture 2, and then incorporate the images into your website. To learn more about Adobe Photoshop products, visit the Adobe website (adobe.com).

If you're not interested in becoming your own photographer, but you'd like to incorporate original photos on your website that you own the rights to, consider hiring a professional photographer to take your photos. You can find local photographers listed in the telephone book or by using a service such as Guru.com or eLance.com. Plan on spending at least several hundred dollars to have a professional photographer create a selection of images in digital format.

Company's Logo

A company logo is typically a single or multicolored graphic image that establishes a visual icon to represent a company. A logo can also be a specific font or typestyle that spells out your company name. Having a visually appealing logo helps establish credibility and recognition, and it helps set your company apart from its competition.

Once you have a company logo created, you want to showcase it prominently on your website, especially in the masthead area. A logo can be created on a computer using graphics software, or it can be hand-drawn by an artist or graphic designer. Ultimately, the logo will need to be transformed into a digital image in order to be incorporated into your website as well as your company letterhead, business cards, ads, and brochures.

Because your logo is an essential part of your company's branding and identity, you want it to look professional, be memorable, and be visually appealing. Ideally, you should hire a graphic artist to help you design your company logo. You can find a professional graphic designer who specializes in freelance logo design using a service like Guru.com or eLance.com. Using any internet search engine, you can also use the search phrase, "logo design."

When hiring an artist, make sure she or he is willing to create a handful of potential logo designs for you. You can then narrow down your choices and have one of the designs fine-tuned by the artist to create what you believe is the perfect logo to represent your company. Plan on spending anywhere from $100 to several thousand dollars to have your logo professionally created. Off-the-shelf logo design software designed for amateurs is available, but the results are typically less professional than if a professional graphic designer created your logo.

Putting the Pieces Together

Now that you have the various pieces to your website's puzzle, it's time to put those pieces together to create the most effective website possible, one that's designed to effectively sell your products/services. But before proceeding, make sure you have the following assets and elements ready to go into your website:

- Company logo
- Product/service descriptions
- Product photographs and illustrations and a photo of yourself (if you're offering yourself as a freelancer)
- Additional text elements for your site (company background, FAQs, return policy, guarantee, testimonials, etc.)
- Any multimedia content you plan to add to your site
- A registered website domain name
- A short biography outlining your experience, services offered, education, and overall credentials
- Samples of your work in an online portfolio, if applicable

This part of the website design and publishing process can be done relatively easily, quickly, and inexpensively. However, the more creative you are at making your website easy-to-use, unique, and functional, the easier it will be for you to attract traffic to your site and transform those web surfers into paying customers/clients. Remember, the focus of your site should be to sell your products/services, not show off flashy technology.

Initial Startup Costs

The initial startup costs to launch your online presence will vary greatly, based on a number of factors:

- The cost of your inventory (if applicable)
- How much advertising and marketing you plan to do
- The decisions you make when setting up the infrastructure of your business venture
- How much you spend creating original assets for your website—logos, custom photography, animations, etc.
- Which e-commerce or website turnkey solution you use to create and launch your online presence

In the past, creating and hosting a secure website capable of handling online financial transactions (processing credit card orders, for example) was usually the most costly aspect of launching an online business. Today, thanks to turnkey solutions creating an online presence has become extremely inexpensive and very straightforward.

What you'll need to really focus on, and invest time and money into doing, is properly marketing and advertising your new business in order to generate ongoing traffic to the website.

Generating traffic to a new website and setting an online business apart from its competition is one of the biggest challenges startup online business operators face. Those owners who can do this successfully have a much greater chance of ultimate success. In most cases, success involves a significant financial investment in advertising, marketing, public relations, and promotions—all of which must be geared specifically to your business' primary target audience.

One mistake many first-time business operators make is having a large budget for advertising and marketing but using that money ineffectively by designing poorly conceived campaigns that aren't targeted to the right audience. Spending a fortune on advertising and marketing doesn't guarantee you success. It greatly increases your chances of success, however, if the money you invest is spent properly on designing highly effective ads, for example, and then placing those ads in media that your target audience is exposed to. Advertising, marketing, public relations, and promotions are all skills that people spend years fine-tuning. If you don't possess these skills and don't have experience using them, seriously consider hiring professionals who will be able to generate much better results from your budget than you.

As you calculate your startup budget, you want to allocate as much money as possible for designing and launching the most professional and easy-to-use website possible, and properly marketing the site in order to generate traffic to it. Simply publishing a website on the internet and registering it with the search engines and web directories such as Google and Yahoo! is not enough. But it is an important start, as you'll discover in Chapter 10.

Security

Perhaps the biggest concern among people who shop online is the possibility of credit card fraud and identity theft. If someone visits your website and doesn't feel safe making a purchase, he'll wind up shopping elsewhere. How you design your website and position your company will contribute to its perceived credibility among those visiting your website for the first time. However, when it comes right down to it, in addition to showcasing yourself as a reliable, trustworthy, and legitimate business, you'll also need to put proper online security measures in place to protect your business as well as your customers.

Your website hosting service, e-commerce turnkey solution provider, and/or your credit card merchant account provider are able to assist you in incorporating adequate online security measures into your website to prevent credit card fraud and other security-related problems. Although you can cut corners and eliminate some of these security precautions, doing so will open you up to potential legal liabilities and decrease your credibility among customers.

For an e-commerce website to be considered safe and secure, it must be able to offer secure transactions using the Secure Electronic Transaction Protocol (SET), the Secure Sockets Layer (SSL) protocol, or another form of encryption and online security that allows you, the website operator, to accept and process credit card information and personal data from your clients without that data being compromised or inadvertently made available to the general public or hackers.

If you're using a turnkey solution to host your website, chances are that all of the necessary security is either already built in or available at an additional fee. VeriSign is the leading source for secure sockets layer (SSL) Certificate Authority, which enables secure e-commerce and communications for websites, intranets, and extranets. The company secures more than 500,000 web servers worldwide with strong encryption and rigorous authentication.

According to VeriSign, "Without SSL encryption, packets of information travel through networks in full view. Imagine sending mail through the postal system in a clear envelope. Anyone with access to it can see the data. If it looks valuable, they might take it or change it. Without third-party verification, how do you know a website is really a business you trust? Imagine receiving an envelope with no return address and a form asking for your bank account number. An SSL Certificate helps website visitors protect sensitive information and get a better idea of who they are trusting with it."

As a website operator, SSL helps you deliver a secure and convenient way for customers to interact with you over the internet. The company reports, "VeriSign is the SSL Certificate provider of choice for over 93 percent of the Fortune 500 and the world's 40 largest banks." By displaying the VeriSign Secured Seal on your site near the online order form or shopping cart, your customers will recognize the most trusted security mark on the internet. To learn more about online security relating to credit card transactions, call (866) 893-6565, or visit the VeriSign website (verisign.com/ssl/ssl-information-center/index.html).

Selecting the Right E-Commerce Turnkey Solution

Every online business has different needs, based on what's being sold, to whom products are being sold, and on what features and functionality the online seller wishes to incorporate into her site. Once you pinpoint what you want and need, finding a complete turnkey solution that meets your requirements at a price you can afford is a relatively straightforward process. The following information covers several popular website and e-commerce turnkey solutions that allow you to design and launch a site quickly, typically within a few hours or a few days.

eBay ProStores

Service provider: eBay.com

Phone number: (866) 747-3229

Website: prostores.com

Turnkey solution pricing: $6.95 to $249.95 per month plus additional fees

As a complete solution, ProStores provides tools to handle everything from website development to inventory management and merchandising. For people just getting started and looking to test their online business idea, the ProStores Express service starts at $6.95 per month with a 1.5 percent per transaction fee on every sale. The Express service allows you to design a basic e-commerce website and get up and running within a few hours, providing you are selling fewer than ten products.

For online business operators with more advanced and extensive needs, eBay offers ProStores Business, ProStores Advanced, and ProStores Enterprise ($29.95, $74.95, and $249.95 per month respectively, with a .50 percent per transaction fee.) With these different plans, online businesses can grow almost limitlessly as needed.

ProStores works seamlessly with eBay Stores and traditional eBay auctions, so merchants can also take advantage of online auctions to sell products. However, the goal of ProStores, like Yahoo! Stores (described later in this chapter), is to provide all the tools an online business operator needs, without requiring them to have any programming or website design skills or experience. All websites are created by fully customizing templates. ProStores, however, offers extreme flexibility when it comes to using these templates, so if you do have programming skills or wish to hire a programmer to modify your site, it's certainly possible.

If your website design needs exceed the online tools available for a fee, ProStores offers a team of professional website designers who can create e-commerce sites from scratch or add full customization to existing templates. A fully functional e-commerce site can be created for a one-time fee of between $399 and $649, depending on the site development package you purchase.

The $649 website design package fully utilizes all of ProStore's capabilities and includes a customized version of the following web pages: Home Page, About Us, Customer Service, Store Location(s), Privacy Policy, FAQ's, Store Policies, an online catalog featuring up to 20 products (adding additional products costs $20 each or you can do it yourself for free), a fully integrated Shopping Cart module, and PayPal and/or online credit card processing functionality (with basic shipping and sales tax calculations). For an additional fee, ProStores will even maintain your site and keep it updated with new content that you provide. Of course, if you don't wish to use the ProStores professionals to design and maintain your website, you can use the online tools provided to do everything yourself or hire your own team of freelance professionals.

According to eBay, "ProStores offers a fully featured web store that can be customized specifically for each online seller. Unlike an eBay Store, ProStores sites are accessed through a URL unique to the seller and have no eBay branding. ProStores sellers are also responsible for driving their own traffic. While items on ProStores sites will sell at fixed prices only, they can also be easily listed onto the eBay Marketplace in either the auction or fixed price formats."

The Business ProStores and above service tiers are fully integrated with many popular online payment gateways and merchant account providers, which means no additional software is required for your online store to accept and process credit card payments with your own merchant account. Some of the merchant account providers ProStores is fully compatible with include: Authorize.net (authorize.net), CyberSource (cybersource.com), Innovative Gateway Solutions (innovativegateway.com), LinkPoint (linkpoint.com), Payflow Pro (paypal.com), and QuickBooks Merchant Services (quickbooks merchantservice.com).

From a bookkeeping and client database management standpoint, ProStores is compatible with several third-party software packages, including QuickBooks from Intuit (quickbooks.com). A variety of online marketing, advertising, and promotional tools are also available.

For startup online businesses and business operators first learning about e-commerce, ProStores offers technical support, easy-to-use tutorials, and a comprehensive set of online tools to handle virtually all aspects of getting your business venture designed, launched, and fully operational. This turnkey solution is ideal for people with little or no programming knowledge. To see several fully operational e-commerce websites that utilize eBay ProStores, visit prostores.com/prostores-featured.shtml.

GoDaddy.com's WebSite Tonight® and Quick Shopping Cart

Service provider: GoDaddy

Website: godaddy.com

Turnkey solution pricing: $9.99 to $49.99 per month plus additional fees

In addition to being a well-established website hosting service and ISP, GoDaddy.com is also an inexpensive domain name registrar and offers a wide range of a la carte online tools for promoting and managing any type of website. For people interested in launching a business that uses an e-commerce site complete with Shopping Cart module, GoDaddy's turnkey solution is called Quick Shopping Cart.

The Quick Shopping Cart application can be fully customized and is compatible with PayPal and some independent credit card merchant accounts. For an additional fee, an online business operator can obtain a merchant account through GoDaddy that allows secure, real-time credit card transactions.

The "Economy" Quick Shopping Cart application ($9.99 per month), which can be used to create a standalone e-commerce site or incorporated seamlessly into any website, allows a product catalog of up to 20 items. The plan includes 50 megabytes of online storage and one gigabyte of monthly bandwidth. The "Deluxe" Quick Shopping Cart ($29 per month) allows a product catalog with up to 100 items and includes one gigabyte of online storage, plus 50 gigabytes of bandwidth per month. In addition, the application can be integrated with QuickBooks.

For those with a large selection of items or plans to expand their offerings over time, GoDaddy's "Premium Edition" Quick Shopping Cart ($49.99 per month) allows unlimited products to be featured and includes two gigabytes of online storage, 100 gigabytes per month of bandwidth, and QuickBooks integration.

GoDaddy's Quick Shopping Cart has secure online transactions and offers a variety of tools to customize the shoppers' experience when they visit your site. The comprehensive selection of tools provided also allows you to properly manage your business, track orders, and market your site. Using this service, you design the look of your store, add products to your catalog, and select shipping, payment, and tax options.

The Quick Shopping Cart can be purchased in conjunction with a wide range of other tools and resources for online business operators, or you can purchase complete turnkey solutions (starting at $155.54 per year) that include website design tools and site hosting using GoDaddy's popular and easy-to-use WebSite Tonight service, the "economy" Quick Shopping Cart, and Traffic Blazer Plus, a suite of tools designed to help you market and promote your business.

There are several different options for establishing your own credit card merchant account through GoDaddy. A Standard Merchant Account allows you to accept orders from the United States only. There's a one-time application fee of $59.95, a monthly fee of $20, a discount rate of 2.59 percent (per transaction), and a per-transaction fee of $.35.

Depending on what you're selling and if you want to accept orders from the United States and Canada, you may need to apply for a Specialty Merchant Account. The application fee is $199. There's also a $20 monthly fee, a discount rate of 2.39 percent (per transaction), and a per-transaction fee of $.30 that's associated with this merchant account.

An International Merchant Account allows you to accept and process credit card orders from virtually anywhere in the world. There's a $695 application fee, plus a $20 per month fee. The discount rate starts at 4.95 percent per transaction, and there's a $.40 per transaction fee.

Merchants receive the funds from credit card orders within 24 to 72 hours, and applications for merchant accounts are typically approved within one day. The merchant account you acquire through GoDaddy works seamlessly with the WebSite Tonight and Quick Shopping Cart applications, and allows secure online payment transactions.

> **CLICK TIP**
>
> GoDaddy.com, along with many other companies, offers a wide range of online tools and resources ideal for designing and publishing traditional websites that don't have an e-commerce (shopping cart) component.

Another nice feature of the Quick Shopping Cart application is that merchants can quickly sell items through eBay auctions (using a special Certified eBay listing tool). GoDaddy offers telephone and online technical support 24/7. Overall, this is one of the more robust and flexible e-commerce turnkey solutions available, and the services are offered at very competitive prices, are easy to use, and required no programming.

OSCommerce

Service provider: OSCommerce

Website: oscommerce.com

Turnkey solution pricing: $ Free (site hosting not included)

If you're looking for extremely powerful and versatile e-commerce website development tools that will allow you to create the most professional and highly functional online business possible, look no further than OSCommerce. Unlike the turnkey solutions described earlier in this chapter, OSCommerce is downloadable software that runs on your computer. It can be used to design, publish, and maintain an e-commerce website.

OSCommerce is not a complete turnkey solution in that it does not offer online hosting services for your online business. It does, however, provide a free collection of development tools. Although this is extremely powerful software, it requires a learning curve and some basic programming knowledge to fully utilize. An alternative is to take advantage of the free OSCommerce website templates available and simply customize them. And because OSCommerce is so popular, you'll have no trouble finding extremely talented programmers with the know-how to fully customize your site using this software. All of the documentation you need to get started is provided free of charge from the OSCommerce website.

According to the software's creators,

> OSCommerce is an online shop e-commerce solution that offers a wide range of out-of-the-box features that allows online stores to be set up fairly quickly with ease, and is available for free as an Open Source-based solution released under the GNU General Public License.
>
> OSCommerce was started in March 2000 and has since matured to a solution that is currently powering more than 13,000 registered live shops around the world. The success of OSCommerce is secured by a great and active community where members help one another out and participate in development issues reflecting upon the current state of the project. You are more than welcome to contribute to the success of OSCommerce by helping out in the realization of the project, by participating in the forums, by donating to the team developers and sponsoring the project, or just by spreading the word!

For a listing of online stores currently operated using OSCommerce, visit shops.oscommerce.com. The OSCommerce software is much more powerful and customizable than many of the turnkey solutions described in this chapter, but it's also more difficult to use, especially if you're not techno savvy.

OSCommerce templates are available from a wide range of sources. Some of these templates, which can be customized to meet your unique needs, are offered free of charge while others are sold by their independent creators. For a freelance graphic designer, creating the selling OSCommerce-compatible templates is a viable business opportunity.

To find OSCommerce templates online, using any internet search engine, such as Yahoo! or Google, enter the search phrase "OSCommerce templates" or visit one of these sites:

- algozone.com
- myoscommercetemplates.com
- oscmax.com
- oscommercecafe.com
- oscommercetemplates.com
- templatemonster.com/oscommerce-templates.php
- templateworld.com/oscommerce.html
- theoscommercestore.com
- tornado-templates.com/oscommerce-templates.php
- websitetemplatedesign.com

CLICK TIP

When hiring a freelance website designer or programmer, try to negotiate a flat fee for the project rather than an hourly fee. Having a flat rate typically saves you money, and helps ensure your project gets completed in a timely manner.

To have an e-commerce website created from scratch using the OSCommerce software, or to have a template fully customized to meet the unique needs of your online business, you can find qualified programmers using a service for finding freelance programmers such as: eLance.com, getafreelancer.com, or Guru.com. Fees vary greatly, so be sure to shop around and carefully evaluate a website designer's portfolio before hiring him.

Yahoo! Stores (Yahoo! Small Business Solutions)

Service provider: Yahoo!

Phone number: (866) 781-9246

Website: smallbusiness.yahoo.com/ecommerce/

Turnkey solution pricing: $39.95 to $299.95 per month (plus additional fees)

If you know anything about the internet or consider yourself to be an accomplished web surfer, you already know that Yahoo! is one of the most popular internet search engines and web directories. As a company, Yahoo! also offers a wide range of other services to internet users. For online business operators, Yahoo! offers its Small Business Services division. The services offered by this division include a robust e-commerce turnkey solution, Yahoo! Stores, as well as search engine marketing/advertising opportunities for promoting your online business.

No matter which of the Yahoo! Stores plans you purchase, you'll be given full access to the service's Store Design tools, which allow you to design a professional looking site using a step-by-step wizard and templates that can be fully customized. Using this solution, you can sell up to 50,000 unique products and maintain your online business with the utmost of ease.

Included with each Yahoo! Stores package is a fully secure Shopping Cart and Checkout application that can also be fully customized. While you can incorporate your own merchant account to be able to accept credit card payments, Yahoo! Merchant Solutions has a partnership with Chase Paymentech and PayPal to offer fully compatible merchant account and online credit card processing options (for an additional fee).

The turnkey solution offered by Yahoo! also features a vast array of tools for marketing your business and driving traffic to your website, and a variety of order processing, inventory management, website traffic reporting, and bookkeeping tools to make fulfilling orders and managing your customers easier and less time consuming.

Through Yahoo! Stores, Yahoo! Merchant Solutions truly offers a comprehensive e-commerce turnkey solution that's affordable, expandable, easy to use, and highly functional when it comes to designing, launching, and operating your online business. Best of all, you can get your online store up and running in hours, using the service's Store Design tools.

As you grow and expand your website beyond the capabilities of the design tools offered, you'll discover that Yahoo! Stores is fully compatible with popular third-party applications, such as Adobe Dreamweaver. Telephone and online technical support is available 24/7.

Yahoo! Stores has three different price plans: the $39.95 per month "Starter Plan," the "Standard Plan" ($99.95 per month) designed for online businesses generating between $12,000 and $80,000 per month, the "Professional Plan" ($299.95 per month) for businesses generating more than $80,000 per month. Depending on the plan you purchase and whether or not you prepay for service, discounts to the monthly fees are offered. Currently thousands of online-based businesses operate using Yahoo! Stores. To see a sampling of these stores and what you could look like, visit smallbusiness .yahoo.com/ecommerce/customerstores.php.

In addition to the monthly fee, Yahoo! Merchant Solutions charges a per transaction fee of between .75 percent and 1.5 percent of each transaction, depending on the plan you select. This added per transaction fee is in addition to any credit card processing fees you must pay. According to Yahoo!, the transaction fee is, "a fee to maintain the infrastructure that supports your e-commerce services and transaction processing. This fee is based on the final price of the product and is not calculated on shipping and taxes. For comparison, some large e-commerce companies spend roughly 5 to 8 percent of their sales to maintain their e-commerce infrastructure. We charge just .75 to 1.5 percent for access to similar e-commerce infrastructure and services of a similar level of quality."

Because Yahoo! Merchant Solutions is so popular, you'll find many independent freelance programmers who can help you customize and design your website, incorporating functionality and features that go beyond what's offered using the supplied Store Design tools. For a listing of pre-approved programming professionals (additional fees apply for their services), visit developernetwork.store.yahoo.com/.

The tools and services offered by Yahoo! Small Business Services are among the most powerful and cost-effective in the industry. You'll find that Yahoo! Merchant Services is equipped to handle the needs of almost every type of online business, yet the tools are easy to use, even for nontechno-savvy people.

Specific Turnkey Solutions for Website Designers

As a website designer, chances are you want to sell your skills and ability to create totally original online content and sites for your clients. Thus, taking advantage of a pre-created website (template) in order to quickly launch your online presence is counterproductive and can hurt your credibility among potential clients/customers. If your business is based on fully customizing website templates for your customers, for example, your online portfolio might showcase multiple, unique variations of specific templates so you can showcase your skills and creativity. However, your own website should be used to set yourself apart from your competition. It should be unique, professional looking, highly functional, and showcase your ability to design and manage a website. After all, as a website designer, your customers will consider your website a sampling of your very best work. Your website must reflect this.

Some of the online services available to freelance professionals, such as Guru.com and eLance.com, allow you to use their online tools to create an online resume and portfolio to showcase your work, to interact with potential clients, and to bid for new jobs. These services can be highly beneficial for freelance website designers (as well as graphic artists and photographers), and are different from launching a standalone website using a template.

Specific Turnkey Solutions for Graphic Artists

There are many ways graphic artists can utilize the web to generate income and freelance business. Many blogging services offer the tools necessary to quickly and easily create online portfolios of your work with absolutely no programming skills required. Likewise, many of the online services designed to match up freelancers with customers/clients also offer the online tools necessary to create a portfolio. Some of these services are eLance.com, ODesk.com, FreelanceDesigners.com, AllGraphicDesign.com, ContractedWork .com, and Guru.com. You might also want to create a website that allows you to sell your designs online and/or use an e-commerce solution so potential customers/clients can hire you via your website to create custom work for them.

Once you determine what business model you want to pursue and what services and/or products you want to offer via your website, you'll be in a much better position to shop around for a turnkey solution to best meet your needs. What's important, however, is that it should be able to showcase examples of your work in the easiest, most visually pleasing and most professional way possible.

Specific Turnkey Solutions for Photographers

As a photographer, you have many options when it comes to generating business and revenue from a website. In addition to using your site as an online portfolio, you can sell prints of your work, interact with potential or existing customers, sell/license stock photography, and/or have products (note cards, T-shirts, mouse pads, mugs, etc.) created and sold using your original photography.

There are dozens of online services specifically for photographers that allow you to create a professional and highly functional website using templates. Many of these services are somehow connected to professional lab services, so prints and other photographic products can be ordered online, allowing you to market your images but have an online service provider handle all order processing, online payments, etc.

You'll want to figure out your main objectives and then choose an online service dedicated to professional and semiprofessional photographers that offers the functionality and price points you're looking for. Just some of the services suitable for professional photographers are listed here. Unlike consumer-oriented photo websites, you'll pay a monthly or annual fee to create and maintain a website using one of these services; however, all of the e-commerce and online portfolio elements are available to you.

Turnkey solutions available to semiprofessional and professional photographers include:

➡ Folio Link—foliolink.com
➡ Photo Identities—photoidentities.com
➡ Pictage—pictage.com
➡ Pictures Pro—picturespro.com
➡ Printroom—printroom.com
➡ Simple Photo—simplephoto.com
➡ Site Welder—sitewelder.com

CLICK TIP

All freelance photographers should have an online portfolio to showcase their work. An example of an online portfolio and website that's set up to sell photos and related products can be found at JasonRichPhotography.com. This site is operated using SmugMug's Professional service.

➡ Sitegrinder—medialab.com/sitegrinder

➡ SmugMug—smugmug.com

Other Website Options for Graphic Artists and Photographers

In addition to using a turnkey solution designed specially for photographers and graphic designers, many creative professionals have developed their online presence (without an e-commerce option) using one of the popular blogging services, such as Blogger.com, WordPress.com, or TypePad.com.

As you create your online presence, simplicity is essential. Visitors to your site should be able to view your work, order prints (or related products), book an appointment with you, view proofs (if applicable), and interact with you online through e-mail. Through your website, potential customers/clients should also be able to learn about you and your credentials via an "About Me" or "Biography" page, and be able to make contact with you easily.

If someone is interested in hiring you as a freelancer, they should be able to do so online. This includes being able to view your pricing, understand what's included, and/or booking an appointment. If booking appointments is one of the objectives of your website, this should be very obvious and easy to do for someone visiting. Likewise, if your goal is to sell your existing work as framed, limited edition prints, for example, this too should be obvious.

Chapter 7

Website Design Fundamentals

*S*avvy web surfers have become accustomed to navigating websites that offer standard types of features and functionality, plus they already know where to look for specific types of content they may be interested in, based on the options offered. This chapter will help you decide what content and functionality should be built into your website, based on what you're trying to accomplish and what target audience you're trying to reach.

Your goal throughout the design process is to create a site that is visually pleasing, extremely easy to navigate, and highly informative. Before you can do this, you must, of course, already know the following information:

- Your website target
- Your products/services
- Your primary marketing message
- The assets available for the site

You then determine specific content you want to incorporate into your site and how that information will be distributed on the various pages. If you surf the web, you'll find virtually all websites share common elements. The most successful also offer a very simple and straightforward layout. All of the information a potential customer could want or need is easy to find and readily available with a few clicks of the mouse.

A well-designed website is a handful of individual web pages. Ultimately, aside from your site's homepage and shopping cart (if applicable), the other pages you incorporate into your site are entirely your choice. This chapter focuses on some of the common content you could incorporate into the various pages of your site as a website professional.

The one word that should be in the forefront of your mind as you design your site is *continuity*. From an overall design, layout, and visual standpoint, each page should fit together nicely and maintain a consistent look, attitude, and tone. For example, you probably want to use the same fonts, typestyles, and color scheme throughout the site.

CLICK TIP

Savvy web surfers spend a lot of time visiting many different websites. They know, for example, that from a website's main page, they can often find information about a company by clicking on the Company Information, About Us, or Company Background icon or menu option. Likewise, as they're reading a product description for something they'd like to order, they already know to click on the Add to Cart or Buy Now icon, to add that item to their shopping cart and begin the ordering process.

It All Starts from the Homepage

When web surfers type your company's URL into their browser or click on a link to your website, your homepage is where they'll wind up. The content of your homepage is the first thing potential customers/clients see, so it's essential that you're able to make a positive first impression extremely quickly. Because look, layout, overall design, and content of your homepage sets the tone for your entire site, thus it should be welcoming and informative, and get the potential customer excited to learn more about what you have to offer. Web surfers have very short attention spans. If they don't find exactly what they're looking for or they don't feel comfortable visiting your site within the first 15 seconds, they'll simply leave and probably won't ever return.

The website template you use to design your site helps you establish a professional-looking layout. However, you ultimately determine what content and information is to be incorporated into your site. These are decisions made based on what you're selling, what message you're attempting to communicate, who your target audience is, and your own personal preferences. Still, your homepage should incorporate the following core elements (listed in alphabetical order):

➡ *Company logo.* This graphic should be displayed prominently at the top of your homepage, as well as on every page of your site. A logo is a unique visual graphic and can, but does not have to, display the company's name. It uniquely identifies your company. Logos are used to help create brand or product awareness.

➡ *Company name.* In text form as well as through the logo, your company's name should appear prominently at the top of your homepage and on all subsequent pages of your site.

➡ *Contact information.* Displayed at least once on every page of your website should be your company's phone number (preferably a toll-free number) as well as your e-mail address so customers know they can reach you with their questions or place their order by telephone if they're not comfortable completing an online order form. Making a phone number available to your customers/clients enhances your companys' credibility and your customer's confidence in it.

- *Copyright and privacy policy information.* At the very bottom of your homepage, in small type, include a copyright notice, trademark information, and a link to your company's privacy policy (if applicable).
- *Navigation bar/menu.* From your site's navigation bar or main menu, the visitor should be able to access all of the important web pages that make up your site.
- *Product categories.* For e-commerce websites, product categories allow a user to search for products by category. If you'll be offering a collection of products, dividing them into categories to display similar products together makes it easier for customers to review offerings of interest to them.
- *Search box.* This feature allows visitors to find exactly what they're looking for by entering a keyword, search phrase, or product number. It can help people quickly find exactly what they're looking for.
- *Specials or promotions box.* Promote your daily or weekly specials. Are you offering a buy one, get one free offer? Perhaps free shipping on orders over $100 or a 10 percent discount if an order is placed by a specific date? Use this portion of your homepage to generate urgency and further build interest in your products.
- *Store/company description.* While the About Us, Biography, or Company Information pages should contain a detailed descriptions of you, your

---

WARNING

Avoid displaying a hit counter on your homepage. This indicates how many people have visited your site since its launch or on a specific day (based on how the counter is set up). While as a business operator, knowing this information is essential, it's not something you want to advertise to your competition or customers. If someone visits your site at 3 p.m. on day and the displayed counter is at 31,503, for example and two days later they revisit your site and the counter is only at 31,510, this indicates very few people have visited your site. This could plant a seed of doubt in a potential customer's mind about your company's popularity and credibility if so few people are visiting and shopping at it.

company, its management, and its history, adding a short, well-written description about you and/or your company on your homepage provides an immediate introduction to your prospective customers/clients and a preview of what they can expect from the site. Keep this to one or two sentences.

Your homepage serves as the main hub for the rest of your site. From here, a visitor should be able to quickly access any content on your site with just one or two clicks of the mouse. From this page, visitors (whether they're web savvy or not) should be able to find product/service information, learn about your company, view your portfolio, discover your company's policies, make contact with you directly, and quickly link to your site's shopping cart so they can place their order with ease (if applicable).

Individual Web Pages

A website is typically divided into a number of individual web pages, or at the very least, offers a bunch of different user options from the main (home) page. Depending on what you're hoping to accomplish with your website, who your target audience is, and what functionality you deem to be essential, the following section outlines common web pages and functionality you should consider offering as part of your website.

When developing your own site, pick and choose the website elements and pages that will be relevant, useful, and offer the greatest functionality, based on your overall objectives. Don't clutter your site with content that isn't relevant or that will confuse your visitors. The following, listed in alphabetical order, are the most common individual web pages that can be incorporated into your site.

➡ *Blog, Podcast, or Newsletter.* One way to enhance customer loyalty, teach people more about your products, increase repeat orders, and build brand awareness is to offer a regularly published (daily, weekly, or monthly) blog, podcast, or downloadable newsletter. You'll want to communicate your marketing message in your blog, podcast, or newsletter, and they should also include information that is valuable to your customers: how-to articles or tips for saving time or money when using your products/services. Use your creativity to provide interesting news. While you can offer these options as free downloads from your website, you can also have an opt-in e-mail list that people subscribe to have your blog, podcast, or newsletter sent directly to their inbox.

➡ *Company Information, About Us, Biography, or Company Background.* Use this page to tell your company's story (or your personal story), explain why your company and its products/services are different from your competitions', and say why your products/services are unique or special. Keep your company/personal information to one page or one screen.

➡ *Contact Us.* One of the most important and powerful ways you can quickly build customers/clients confidence in your business is to make yourself available to answer their questions, address their concerns, and handle their problems. In addition to displaying a toll-free phone number, be sure to display your company's full mailing address and e-mail address. Making your customers feel they can reach you easily if they experience a problem or have questions gives more confidence when placing an order.

➡ *Customer Testimonials.* A page that reproduces actual customer testimonials about your company and its products is a great way to build up customer or client confidence and enhance your credibility. Keep the testimonials short and to the point, but make sure they're positive, believable, accurate, truthful, and informative.

➡ *FAQ.* No matter how straightforward and easy to understand the information about your products/services and your company's policies are, visitors to your website will still have questions about pricing, product specifications, services offered, how to place an order, your return policy, etc. FAQ (Frequently Asked Questions) documents usually adhere to a question and answer format and are used to answer the most common customers/clients questions. Having this information on your site will reduce the amount of direct contacts (via phone or e-mail) you have with customers.

➡ *News, Sales, and Promotions.* This page can be used just like a weekly circular or print advertisement that promotes news about your company and its products/services, and it can promote sales or promotions.

→ *Online Ordering/Shopping Cart.* When a visitor to your website is ready to place an order (if applicable), they'd click on a Buy Now or Order icon and get linked to your site's Shopping Cart. The Shopping Cart is an online order form that allows your customers to input their order-related information, including their payment details, and have the order processed (often in real-time). While the turnkey e-commerce website solution you use will include a shopping cart, it's essential that the application built into your site be easy to use and understand, and include all of the functionality for your customers to quickly and easily place their order online.

→ *Portfolio.* By publishing a sampling of your best work online, you allow potential customers and clients to see what you're capable of first-hand. You can showcase your skills, knowledge, experience, creativity, and ability to meet the unique needs of your customers/clients. It's one thing to tell a potential customer that you're capable of doing something. It's a much more powerful tool, however, to be able to show them specific examples of work you've done in the past that is somewhat similar to their own needs. No matter what type of creative work you do, never underestimate the benefits of incorporating an online portfolio of your work into your website. Your portfolio should set you apart from your competition in a positive way and make it clear you possess the skills, knowledge, and resources necessary to do highly professional work. See Chapter 9 for tips on how to create an awesome online portfolio.

→ *Press Room.* Part of your success strategy should be to use a public relations campaign to generate publicity about your business and its products in the media. The Press Room area of your website should contain an online press kit, copies of press releases, high-resolution product photography (if applicable), and contact information for members of the media (reporters, journalists, and editors) to reach you quickly. When members of the media are working on stories, they're typically under very tight deadlines. If you make all of the information they need available to them on your site, your chances of receiving free publicity and having your products mentioned in articles, features, or news stories increases dramatically. The Press Room area of your website can also be used to showcase publicity you've already received.

➡ *Product/Service Descriptions.* For an e-commerce website, product/service descriptions and/or catalog pages are absolutely essential. It's here your customers/clients will learn about the products and services you're offering through detailed, well-written descriptions and applicable photography. You want to keep your product/service descriptions relatively short, but they must also be comprehensive, informative, accurate, and easy to understand. All your descriptions should be consistent in format and tone, and should be targeted specifically to your primary audience. In conjunction with each description, you'll want to include a "Buy," "Order," or "Add to Cart" icon, so customers can quickly place their orders online.

CLICK TIP

To help improve your Search Engine Optimization efforts, product descriptions should appear on your website as text whenever possible, not as part of graphic elements. Text allows search engine spiders or crawlers to easily find, categorize, and catalog your site's content appropriately, which in turn helps boost your search engine placement and rankings on most popular search engines.

➡ *Return Policy/Guarantee/Warrantee.* Displaying this information for your customers/clients helps boost their confidence before they place their order. An important aspect of good customer service is explaining up front how your company handles problems and a customer's need or desire to return products. If you charge a restocking fee for returns or issue refunds within 15 days, these policies should all be spelled out on your site. Keep in mind, your customers/clients will appreciate a 30-day, no-questions-asked, unconditional return policy that has no restocking fee. The easier it is for a customer to handle returns, the more confident they'll be in taking a chance and buying your products, sight unseen, from your website. If your products/services come with a guarantee or warrantee, this should also be well promoted on your site to boost customer confidence.

➡ *Splash Page.* Some websites use a fancy opening animation to introduce people to their website. Such introductions are called *Splash Pages*, because they're supposed to make a splash when someone sees it. The goal is to generate a wow effect. The problem with Splash Pages is that they look great but take valuable time to load and typically say absolutely nothing about the company or its products. In other words, for most websites, they're an utter waste of time. If a potential customer has to wait even five seconds for a site's Splash Page to load, you run a great risk of losing them before they've even visited your site. Remember, your potential customers are visiting your site to learn about and/or buy a product/service, not to be entertained by a fancy graphic animation sequence before they're permitted to visit your real homepage.

➡ *Technical Support/Customer Service.* Depending on what you're selling, it may be necessary or appropriate to offer ongoing technical support to existing customers via telephone, online (through live chats), or via e-mail. Having an area dedicated to helping customers use your products once they order them improves customer loyalty, generates repeat orders, and increases your chances of receiving positive word-of-mouth advertising. One of your business's goals should be providing the most professional, helpful, friendly, and accessible customer service possible. In some cases, customers will go out of their way or pay

---

WARNING

Many website operators and bloggers are intrigued that they can generate additional revenue from their websites by displaying ads. If your website is designed to be showcase your work as a professional website designer, graphic artist, or photographer, that's all it should do. You don't want to distract potential customers/clients by displaying ads for other companies, products, or services.

more for products/services if they know they'll be supported by top-notch customer service or technical support from the company they make the purchase from.

Know Your Customer's Surfing Capabilities

Not all web surfers access the internet using a high-speed connection (DSL, broadband, or FIOS). According to Leichtman Research Group, in July 2007, of U.S. homes with internet access around 47 percent (33 million users) still use the slow dial-up connection. The Leichtman Research Group reports, "Broadband adoption is affected by household income. Broadband reaches 68 percent of households with annual incomes over $50,000. By contrast, 39 percent of households with incomes under $50,000 subscribe to broadband services."

Make sure your site (or a version of your site) works well for people using a slow internet connection. Also, avoid incorporating features into your site that require browser plug-ins that aren't common. Many web surfers have added a Flash player and/or PDF file reader plug-in to their browser, but there are plenty of plug-ins that are far less popular.

CLICK TIP

Thanks to improving technologies, lower prices, and the growing popularity of the internet, Jupiter Research reports that adoption of high-speed internet services is expected to reach 70 percent of all U.S. households by 2012.

If your site requires the use of a less popular plug-in, you will greatly reduce the number of web surfers capable of visiting and ordering from your site. Focus on catering to the broadest audience possible, unless you know that the majority of people in your target audience are web savvy and utilize a high-speed connection.

Test Before Launching Your Site

As an online businessperson, you're probably too close to the project emotionally to maintain proper prospective when it comes to determining if your site's content truly appeals to its target audience and has achieved its objective. One way to ensure you're achieving your objective—to create the most welcoming, informative, and easy-to-navigate site possible—is to invite friends, co-workers, potential customers/clients, and just people you know to explore your site before it's officially published and launched. Solicit detailed feedback from these people.

The following are 25 sample questions to ask your website testers to help you improve your website before it actually launches:

1. Is the website visually appealing?
2. Is the website easy to understand?
3. Were you able to find product/service information quickly and easily?
4. Were you able to find and use the Shopping Cart without confusion?
5. Would you order from this company with confidence?
6. What would you incorporate into the site to make it more welcoming, informative, or easier to use?
7. How would you compare this site with our competition, and other sites you've visited in the past?
8. Based on what you've learned from our site, what would you say is the most important or useful information about our products/services?
9. Did you find any errors or typos on the website?
10. Do the photos featured on the site reveal enough detail about what we're selling?
11. Based on your experience surfing around other sites, what elements or features is our site lacking?
12. Did we incorporate too much, too little, or just the right amount of information and content on each individual web page in the site?
13. Did you find our homepage welcoming and informative?
14. Do you believe our company's policies, guarantees, and warrantees are fair and easy to understand?
15. Did you feel confident in your ability to reach our customer service department via telephone, e-mail, or online chat to get your questions answered or your concerns addressed?
16. At any point did you get lost or confused? If so, where and why?
17. Are our product/service descriptions accurate and detailed enough?
18. Did you find any of the product/service descriptions misleading in anyway?

19. From a readability standpoint, is all of the text on the site easy to read? Is the text too small, too large, or too cluttered? Are the fonts, typestyles, text colors, and/or background colors visually appealing or distracting?

20. In your opinion, what is the best and worst feature of the website overall?

21. Are our prices competitive?

22. After visiting the site for the first time, would you be likely to place an order right away, or would you first shop around and compare us to our competitors?

23. What is one feature or piece of content on the website that you would change to make it better? How would you improve it?

24. Is there any information about our company or our products that you could not easily and quickly find on the site? If so, what?

25. What would prevent you from placing an order on our website during your first visit?

The people you ask to test your site should not necessarily be familiar with your products, but they should be people whom you perceive to be your potential customers. They should not have a technical background. In other words, find people who are not programmers or professional website designers. You want everyday web surfers to explore your site and offer their honest feedback.

CLICK TIP

Check out what works for other websites. Thanks to statistics and information that's published about other e-commerce websites, you can easily determine what works well and what doesn't simply by visiting and learning from the most successful e-commerce websites. Obviously, you'd also want to avoid the mistakes made by the least successful sites. *Internet Retailer* magazine publishes a list of the top 500 retail websites each year (internetretailer.com/top500/list.asp).

Chapter 8

Online Payment Options

*A*s a freelancer and online business operator, you'll need to accept payment for your services as well as for any products you'll be selling. If you're working with customers or your clients in person, you can accept cash or a check as payment. If you'll be dealing with customers and clients online, however, you'll definitely need to acquire a credit card merchant account or use one of the online payment services, such as Google Checkout or PayPal Express Checkout, which allow you

CLICK TIP

If you'll be finding freelance jobs exclusively through services like Guru.com or eLance.com, payment for your work is made through these services, so having a merchant account is probably not needed.

to accept credit card and debit card payments online. Your customers want the convenience and security associated with making their purchases using their credit card, just as they would if they shopped at traditional retail stores.

Merchant Accounts

The need to accept credit card payments requires you to acquire a *merchant account* through a bank or financial institution. To do so typically means paying an application fee, filling out lots of paperwork, and then paying a per-transaction fee plus a small percentage of each credit card sale to the merchant account provider. If you'll be operating an online business, your merchant account provider must also provide resources that are compatible with your website hosting company so credit card orders can be processed securely and in real-time online.

It's important to shop around for the best deal when looking for a merchant account because fees vary dramatically. In addition to contacting local banks, do a search on Google or Yahoo! using the search phrase "Merchant Account." You should also contact your website hosting company because most already have partnerships with merchant account providers, which makes it easier for you to get started accepting credit card payments. Whatever fees you wind up paying to accept credit card payments must be calculated into your cost of doing business. It may be necessary to forward some of these costs onto your customers by raising your prices slightly for the products/services you'll be selling.

Most merchant account providers can set you up with the ability to accept Visa, MasterCard, Discover, and American Express payments, as well as debit card payments and electronic check payments. The fees, however, may be different for each credit card or payment type. For example, depending on the merchant account provider, you may wind up paying a higher per-transaction fee and/or discount rate for an order paid for using an American Express card than for a debit card.

As a business operator, you need to determine the fastest, most convenient, and most cost-effective ways you can be paid for your products/services. In many cases, this will involve being able to accept credit card (Visa, MasterCard, American Express, or Discover) payments from your customers and clients. To do this, however, you'll probably want to establish a credit card merchant account with a bank, financial institution, or credit card merchant account provider, although you can also accept credit card payments if you register for services like PayPal or Google Checkout.

If you're dealing with customers in person, you can easily accept cash, traveler's checks, or personal/company checks for purchases, in addition to debit cards and credit cards. If you'll be operating an online business, however, you'll want to be able to accept credit cards and debit cards, and make the online payment process as quick and easy as possible for your customers and clients.

This chapter explores how to establish a credit card merchant account, so you can begin accepting major credit card and debit card payments from your customers and clients.

The following are five strategies for obtaining a merchant account:

1. *Compare prices carefully and watch out for hidden and recurring fees.* Most merchant account providers charge a percentage of each sale, called the discount rate, in addition to a fixed per-transaction fee. Additional fees you'll want to compare are the application fees for setting up the account and any recurring monthly fees that you'll be required to pay in order to maintain the account and be able to accept credit card payments. You may be offered a lower discount rate by one provider, but that same provider will have a higher per-transaction fee or a higher than average recurring monthly fee. Other potential fees to watch out for are associated with having to purchase or lease credit card processing equipment and/or software.

2. *For a startup company with no sales track record, negotiating for lower rates from a merchant account provider is a challenge.* However, once you develop

a relationship with your merchant account provider and demonstrate a track record of growing monthly sales, you could go back and try to negotiate a lower per transaction fee and/or discount rate. Even a small reduction to your discount rate will save you a fortune over time and instantly increase your profit margin on whatever you're selling.

3. *The contract you'll be required to sign with your merchant account provider will probably be a complex and confusing legal document.* Before signing it, understand exactly what you're agreeing to in terms of the fees and the duration of the contract. If you sign a two-year agreement, for example, but your business only remains open for six months, you'll still be required to pay the minimum monthly fees for the duration of the contracted agreement (or pay a hefty cancellation fee).

4. *Make sure the merchant account provider you choose offers the tools and resources necessarily to seamlessly integrate credit card processing into your website (through your website hosting service).* A lack of compatibility can cause tremendous headaches and cost you extra to get everything to work properly. Ease of implementation and security are important factors to consider.

5. *Not all merchant account providers are alike.* In addition to charging different fees, each offers its own level of customer service and technical support. You also need to know how quickly transactions will be processed so you know when the money from incoming credit card sales is deposited into your bank account. How long this takes (between a few hours and several days) varies among merchant account providers.

As a small business operator, there are a number of reasons to acquire a merchant account and be able to accept major credit cards and debit cards as payment from your customers:

➡ Accepting credit cards increases impulse buying. Studies have proven that merchants who accept credit cards can increase sales by up to 50 percent.

➡ If you have your own merchant account, you can typically accept credit card payments online, over the telephone, by mail, or in person.

➡ You can sell products/services on an installment basis by obtaining permission to charge your customers' or clients' credit card monthly, or as per agreement.

➡ Processing time is relatively quick, and money is often deposited in your bank account within 48 hours.

➡ You can ship products knowing you have been paid in full and do not have to worry about CODs, bum checks, or slow payers.

Merchant accounts also pose some problems for small businesspeople:

➡ It can be costly to set up and maintain a credit card merchant account, including:

· Setup and application fees	$0 to $1,000
· Equipment and software purchases	$200 to $1,000
· Equipment and software leases	$25 to $100 per month
· Administration and statement fees	$10 to $100 per month
· Processing fees	2 to 8 percent of total sales
· Transaction fees	$.15 to $.50 per transaction

➡ Credit card companies can hit you with stiff "chargeback fees" for goods returned and credits returned to customers' credit card accounts.

➡ If you're not careful and fail to follow your merchant account's policies exactly, you could become responsible for fraudulent credit card transactions perpetrated by your customers/clients.

The Online Payment Process

The primary difference between an ordinary website and an e-commerce site is that the latter accepts online orders and is designed to be an online business, not just a marketing or promotional tool or vehicle for disseminating information.

When someone places an order from your site, depending on the online payment services made available to them, they can complete their purchases and initiate payment using one of the following options:

- Submit credit card, debit card, or electronic check information online, assuming the seller has a merchant account and is able to accept Visa, MasterCard, American Express, and/or Discover.
- Call your company's (toll-free) phone number and place the order via telephone.
- Mail in a personal or company check.
- Request to have the order shipped COD or charged against their credit line with your company via purchase order.
- Wire money between the Buyer and Seller's bank accounts.
- Google Checkout or PayPal.

Your goal as an online merchant is to create a shopping experience that's quick, convenient, secure, and straightforward. The fewer mouse clicks and data entry someone has to do to complete their order, the better. During the design phase of your site, pinpoint exactly the information you need to collect from your customers during the order-taking process. Next, determine the quickest and most efficient way to collect that information, which will probably include:

- Purchaser name
- Billing address
- Recipient name
- Shipping address
- Customer phone number
- Customer e-mail address,

CLICK TIP

Ideally, you'll want to provide your customers with the option to have their basic information saved so when they return to your site to place future orders, they don't need to re-enter all of their personal information. From a merchant's standpoint, this functionality is added using cookies, a concept familiar to all website designers. Cookies may or may not be offered as part of your website turnkey solution.

➡ Name on the buyer credit card

➡ Actual credit card number, expiration date, and the three-digit security code

➡ Details about the item(s) the customer wishes to order (quantity, item name, item number, size, color, etc.).

WARNING

If it takes customers too long to make their purchases on your website or the check out process is too confusing, they'll quickly become frustrated and shop elsewhere. As an online merchant, your goal is to transform as many visitors to your site into paying customers/clients as is possible. When calculated as a percentage, the number of visitors to your site who actually make a purchase (versus leave without making a purchase) is referred to as your "conversion rate." When a consumer/client visits your site, starts the buying process, but ultimately decides against making the purchase, that's referred to as "cart abandonment." Offering an express checkout process, through Google Checkout or PayPal Express Checkout, reduces cart abandonment for many online merchants.

Alternate Online Payment Options

To make shopping online a more secure and faster experience to all consumers, both Google and PayPal have developed services that allows consumers to create a single password-protected account and enter all of their personal and financial information just once.

When participating consumers make an online purchase with any participating online merchant, they need only to click on the Google Checkout or PayPal Express Checkout icon that's incorporated into the site's Shopping Cart. They are then seamlessly transferred to either the Google or PayPal system, which already has their name, address, and credit card data stored so there is no need for people to repeatedly enter this information when they place orders with participating merchants.

A consumer can feel safer using Google Checkout, for example, because the merchant they're shopping with never actually receives personal credit card information. Instead, Google processes the payment and then pays the merchant. The consumer also doesn't need to remember user names and passwords for every online merchant he shops with. At anytime, he can review his purchase history, track orders and deliveries, or contact merchants he's done business with—all from one centralized website operated by Google or PayPal.

Using Google Checkout or PayPal is totally free for buyers. They can set up their own secure account in minutes, and there is no extra charge associated with making purchases. It is the merchant that pays fees to use the services.

Theoretically, an online merchant could accept major credit card, debit card, and electronic check payments using either of these services and not have a separate merchant account. However, if customers have not set up Google Checkout or PayPal accounts (and do not wish to do so), they would not be able to place an online order from your site.

The number of consumers who have either a Google Checkout or PayPal account is growing quickly, but as of early 2008, no online merchant should depend only on these payment options. Currently, offering either or both of these online payment options is basically an optional convenience merchants can extend to their customers/clients.

In early 2008, PayPal boasted a network of 150 million active accounts, with 104,500 new accounts opened every day. Google Checkout is a newer service, but it is being actively marketed it to both consumers and merchants in hopes of making it a widely accepted standard for online payments. PayPal accepts foreign currencies, so you can immediately begin tapping the worldwide market with your online business. In fact, PayPal reports it accepts payments in 16 currencies and allows merchants to sell to shoppers in 190 countries and regions. For the consumer, their Google Checkout or PayPal account can store an unlimited number of shipping addresses and credit cards.

Google Checkout

Launched in June 2006, Google Checkout is much newer than PayPal, but it carries the Google brand name and is quickly becoming a popular way for people to pay for their online purchases. One of the many ways Google is attracting customers to sign up for Google Checkout is to offer an ongoing array of money-saving offers and promotions when the service is used. For example, during the 2007 holiday season, customers earned two frequent flier miles (on the airline of their choice) per dollar spent using Google Checkout. Other holiday promotions included free shipping from participating merchants or an instant savings of $10 to $50 off their online order(s).

For merchants, one benefit of Google Checkout is that they can use the Google Checkout logo or shopping cart logo in their online advertising, including within Google AdWords ads. This instantly identifies your online business as supporting Google Checkout, so your potential customers know they can expect a quick, secure, and easy online shopping experience. Thousands of well-known merchants and plenty of startups currently support Google Checkout. For a partial listing of merchants, visit google.com /checkout/m.html.

Unlike PayPal, Google Checkout is a "checkout flow," not a form of payment or person-to-person money transfer service. When someone makes a payment using Google Checkout, they're ultimately paying with the major credit card that's on file with the service. According to Google, "The goal of Google Checkout is to help you offer your buyers a fast, safe, and convenient buying experience, not to replace any existing payment types your buyers use."

Currently, Google Checkout is designed to be used by online merchants for transactions involving tangible and digital goods (including downloadable products), however, payments can also be processed for services or subscriptions, as long as all transactions adhere to Goggle's stated content policies. In early 2008, the fees to merchants for Google Checkout were 2 percent of each sale, plus a $.20 per transaction fee. There are no monthly fees, set-up charges, or gateway service fees. Depending on the deal you have with your merchant account provider, these rates are extremely competitive. There are a few other fees and charges an online merchant should be aware of. For example, if a consumer initiates a chargeback, the merchant will be responsible for a $10 chargeback fee. One potential drawback is that Google Checkout only accepts U.S. funds, so it won't work for international sales.

As an online merchant, once you register to accept Google Checkout payments, you'll be able to add a Google Checkout icon to your shopping cart.

CLICK TIP

Google maintains an official Google Checkout Blog for merchants. It can be accessed free of charge by visiting googlecheckout.blogspot.com. Here, you'll find a vast amount of information about how merchants can best use this service to improve sales and profits.

This icon is available in three sizes. It should be placed next to every existing checkout button currently on your site.

For online merchants using a shopping cart application offered by one of dozens of different third-party companies, integrating Google Checkout into your site takes just minutes. For a current list of compatible shopping cart applications, visit checkout.google.com/seller/integrate_getnew.html. If your site has been custom-created, Google offers the necessary tools (for free) to quickly integrate Google Checkout. Visit checkout.google.com/seller/developers.html for details.

PayPal Express Checkout

According to PayPal, in 2008, "Account holders transact an average of over $8.1 billion USD through PayPal every quarter. That's $2 million USD per hour, and over $48 million USD per day. Plus, over $750 million USD is stored in PayPal accounts, which is turned over every two weeks. Stored balances encourage impulse purchases and increased buying . . . Over 80 percent of users say they're more likely to buy from an online business a second time if that business accepts PayPal . . . With the PayPal Express Checkout button on your site, you can increase sales by 14 percent on average. Express Checkout conversion is 40 percent higher than other checkouts."

Unlike Google Checkout, PayPal allows online shoppers to set up a free account and make online payments via a major credit card, debit card, or electronic check. It's also possible for people to maintain a balance in a PayPal account and make purchases using funds from that account.

Like Google Checkout, online merchants can easily incorporate a PayPal Express Checkout feature to the Shopping Cart of their site. Using this feature, customer do not need to re-enter their address and credit card information in conjunction with each purchase. When your customers/clients complete the Shopping Cart on your site, they'd click on the PayPal Express

Check Out icon, instead of your site's regular Check Out icon. They'll be instantly forwarded to the PayPal site, where they simply enter their username and password, select a ship-to address and billing address, and process their payment with a click of the mouse. They then return to your site for confirmation of their order. The process takes just seconds, and as the merchant, you immediately receive the funds in your own PayPal account, which can be linked to your bank account.

For merchants, PayPal makes it easy to create your own customized shopping cart that's compatible with Express Check Out. You can also easily incorporate Buy Now, Add To Cart, View Cart, Donate, or Subscribe buttons within your site.

To begin accepting PayPal payments as a merchant, you'll need to set up either a Business or Premier account with PayPal (visit the paypal.com website and click on the 'Selling with PayPal' link). Currently, more than 100,000 e-commerce websites accept PayPal payments.

If you're creating your website from scratch, upon signing up with PayPal as a merchant, you can select a third-party Shopping Cart for your site that has PayPal integrated into it (using website Payments Standard), or use the directions provided for incorporating PayPal into your own Shopping Cart application. For information about PayPal's compatibility with the various e-commerce turnkey solutions, call PayPal Integration Support at (888) 221-1161.

As a merchant, signing up for a PayPal account takes just minutes, but processing your bank account information will take three to five business days. Using PayPal website Payments Pro (paypal.com/pro) allows you to accept credit cards directly on your website, even if the customer does not have a PayPal account. This plan offers the same functionality as having a traditional credit card merchant account. For this service, you'll pay an ongoing $30 per-month fee, plus a 2.2 to 2.9 percent fee per order, in addition to a $.30 per transaction fee. (The $.30 fee applies to each credit card authorization attempt.)

The website Payments Standard plan from PayPal has no monthly fee, a 1.9 to 2.9 percent fee per sale, plus a $.30 per transaction fee. This plan requires customers to be transferred to the PayPal site and have a PayPal account to make a purchase. Using either plan as a merchant, once you've been a PayPal member for more than 90 days and your sales volume is greater than $3,000 per month, you become eligible for lower fees per transaction. To set up this type of PayPal merchant account, call (866) 836-1648, or visit the PayPal.com website. Regardless of which plan you sign up for as a merchant, there are no set-up fees and no cancellation fees. There's also no minimum contract length, common when you set up a traditional credit card merchant account.

CLICK TIP

E-commerce sites set up using a turnkey solution, such as Yahoo! Stores, eBay ProStores, or GoDaddy.com's Quick Shopping Cart, for example, have built-in PayPal integration, so adding this functionality to your site takes just minutes. Many of these services also offer Google Checkout compatibility (or plan to add it in the near future).

Chapter 9

Creating an Online Portfolio

$\mathcal{A}$s a freelance website designer, graphic artist, or photographer, your ability to land new jobs and build your freelance business online or in the real world will be determined primarily by the quality of your work. If your work is amazing and you market yourself properly, you'll wind up with a vast client base and plenty of work.

The very best way to show off your best work and showcase your skills is to develop a kick-ass online portfolio. Depending on the business model you plan to follow, your portfolio can be part of your own website, a stand-alone website, and/or on an online freelance service such as Guru.com or eLance.com. You can use a turnkey solution for online portfolio creation and management.

Creating a stand-alone website from scratch is probably your best option if you want to create an online presence that's truly unique and that offers an overall design and layout that allows you to fully customize your content and cater it to your potential clients and customers.

A less time-consuming and lower cost option is to utilize a turnkey solution, which is an online-based set of website development tools that allows you to create a customized website using professionally designed templates that you add your own content to. While using a turnkey solution allows you to create a professional looking online presence that is fully functional, the template is not exclusively yours, meaning that a similar looking website could be created by other businesses (including your competition).

CLICK TIP

Your online portfolio should expand on your written resume by showcasing exactly what you can do and provide real-life examples of your work. It's one thing to state you're capable of doing something in a resume or bio. It's another thing altogether to be able to prove it. Your portfolio provides tangible proof of your capabilities, talents, and skills.

Regardless of what methods you use to create and manage your online portfolio, the portfolio itself must:

➡ Showcase your very best work
➡ Showcase work that is of interest to your target audience
➡ Be extremely professional looking and visually appealing (as well as easy to navigate)
➡ Position you as an expert or specialist in your field
➡ Demonstrate that you have the skills, knowledge, and experience of interest to potential clients

➡ Help you set yourself apart from your competition

Determining the right amount of work to showcase in your online portfolio is a personal decision. If you show too little of your work, you will look inexperienced and potential clients won't be able to properly judge your skills. Thus, it'll be harder for them to compare your work to your competition and make an intelligent hiring decision.

CLICK TIP

Depending on the business model you're following, it might also make sense for you to create a traditional portfolio that you can show off to potential clients during in-person meetings.

If, however, you showcase too much of your work, it will take too long for potential clients to review it and it could be confusing, lack focus, or be overwhelming for the viewer. Most potential clients review many portfolios and won't invest too much time looking at any one of them. So, if you don't capture a prospective client's attention within the first few seconds via your portfolio, your chance of getting hired drops dramatically.

Unlike a traditional portfolio, an online portfolio offers you a tremendous opportunity to truly showcase your work, demonstrate your skills, and tap your creativity. Using text, graphics, animations, audio, video, and other multimedia content, you have the ability to harness the power of the internet to create a portfolio that works for you 24 hours per day, 7 days per week, 365 days per year. Not only can your online portfolio show people your work and

CLICK TIP

When people set out to hire a freelance website designer, graphic artist, or photographer, chances are they already have a vision in their mind about what they want created and how they want it to look. Their goal is to find a freelancer whose creative vision and taste are close to their own. This means finding someone who can demonstrate they have the experience, knowledge, and skills to create exactly what the client is looking for—within budget and on time. Design your online portfolio to help these potential clients quickly realize that you are the person they need to hire.

help you demonstrate your skills and experience, it can also help you show off your personality, creativity, and potential.

Online Portfolio Options

When it comes to creating your online portfolio, there are a variety of tools and resources available to you. These tools will help you create an online portfolio that looks professional and uses an easy-to-navigate interface, but the content of your portfolio must be determined by you. The collection of work you showcase will convey a distinct message about you, the quality of your work, your experience, your creativity, your level of professionalism, and your uniqueness. Only when you have determined what work you want to showcase within your portfolio, should you choose the online tools and resources to create, publish, and maintain your portfolio.

A Stand-Alone Online Portfolio

A stand-alone online portfolio is one that is really its own website, with its own URL (website address). The goal of the site is exclusively to showcase your work. There are countless website design tools available, even if you know nothing about website programming, to help you build your online portfolio. See Chapter 6 for information about some of the website turnkey solutions and tools available to you.

Incorporating Your Portfolio into a Website

If you already have an established website or e-commerce site but are looking to expand your online presence to include an online portfolio to generate additional freelance business, adding a portfolio is as easy as designing a few additional web pages and incorporating them into your site. Or, you can use a stand-alone online portfolio creation tool or service and add prominent links to that service within your existing website. From a design standpoint, if you already have an established website, your online portfolio should integrate seamlessly into the existing site in terms of appearance and user interface.

Turnkey Online Portfolio Solutions

There are a variety of specialty services and website templates designed for website professionals to help them create an online portfolio. Some of these services are extremely inexpensive and offer limited functionality, while others are designed to be fully customizable. For example, if you want to showcase digital artwork or photographs, Apple's Mobile Me service (formally dot-Mac) allows Mac users to create online portfolios or galleries of their work with ease. The Portfolios.com website also offers online tools for creating an online portfolio to showcase your work. Many of the specialty online photo websites also allow the creation of basic online portfolios with ease and for very little money. The SmugMug service (smugmug.com) described in Chapter 6 is just one example of a specialty online service for graphic designers and photographers that can be used not just to showcase a portfolio but also as an e-commerce solution.

A truly professional-looking online portfolio that is feature-packed, yet totally customizable to best showcase your work is available from SellFolio (sellfolio.com). This service allows you to select one of more than a dozen templates; add your own photos, artwork, or content; and then publish a fully animated online portfolio that can also be burned to CDs and distributed to potential clients. SellFolio requires no programming skills or knowledge, yet allows a fully customized portfolio to be created around any of the services templates. These templates use graphics, animation, text, original music, and sound, along with your own content, to create a memorable online portfolio.

Below are just a few of the many online companies with tools and resources to help web designers, graphic artists, and photographers create, publish, and manage top-notch, stand-alone portfolios using their own URL:

- ➡ Big Black Bag—bigblackbag.com
- ➡ Colorflot—colorflot.com
- ➡ FolioLink—foliolink.com

CLICK TIP

Choose a service that allows you to create a stunning online portfolio as well as keep track of traffic or visitors to your site. Tracking allows you to better gauge how effective your online portfolio is and to determine what aspects of your portfolio are most interesting to potential clients (visitors).

- → FolioSnap—foliosnap.com
- → IFP3 Creative Photo Solutions—ifp3.com
- → ImpactFolios—impactfolios.com
- → IVwebsites—ivwebsites.com
- → Pictage—pictage.com
- → Pixpa Blue—pixpablue.com

CLICK TIP

All online portfolio creation services offer samples of portfolios. Take a look at them to get ideas on how to best create your own portfolio and to determine whether or not the specific service you're looking at offers the functionality you want and need at a price you can afford.

Adding Your Portfolio to Online Services for Freelancers

If you plan to use an online service such as Guru.com or eLance.com to solicit new freelance business, it's important to use the online portfolio functionality these sites offer to showcase your work. Once you become a member, each of these services provides the online tools for a basic online portfolio. It's included with your membership. While you can (and should) also have a stand-alone online portfolio, many companies that hire freelancers from these services prefer to view online portfolios that are part of the service to save themselves time and because they're already familiar with the user interface. So, if you plan to solicit freelance business using a service like Guru.com or eLance.com, take the time to publish a sampling of your best work as an online portfolio on the service you choose to use.

Ten Tips for Creating an Attention-Getting Online Portfolio

Plan on investing significant time in designing your online portfolio and in determining what work to showcase. Once the portfolio is created, fine-tune and improve it on an ongoing basis so that it perfectly caters to your target audience. Doing so allows it to achieve its primary objective, impressing people enough so they hire you as a freelancer.

Because you want your online portfolio to showcase you and your work in a way that will truly impress a potential customer/client, and convince them to hire you based on your proven skills, talent, and qualifications, it's

CLICK TIP

The interviews featured in Chapter 14 include additional tips and strategies for creating an amazing and attention-getting online portfolio that can be used to impress potential clients and increase business.

important that your portfolio achieve its objective, based on what you're selling and to whom you're selling. The following ten tips will help you design the best possible online portfolio.

Tip #1: Choose Your Focus

As a creative professional, you're probably capable of creating many different types of work. Promoting yourself as a jack of all trades, however, is a definite way to ensure you'll get lost in the shuffle as potential clients search for a freelancer capable of completing a very specific type of job, project, or assignment.

While you want your portfolio to showcase your best work, it should also obviously demonstrate your proficiency and expertise in doing a specific type of work, based on what you decide your specialty will be. Everything you decide to showcase within your portfolio, including your biography, should focus on demonstrating your talent and specialty.

Within 5 to 15 seconds of accessing your portfolio, the viewer should understand exactly what your specialty or focus is, and be able to determine if your skills are along the lines of what she's looking for.

The first step in creating an awesome portfolio is to determine its purpose. Ask yourself questions like:

➡ Why are you creating this portfolio?
➡ Who should it appeal to?
➡ What is the primary message you want the portfolio to convey?

➡ What do you want people to think after reviewing your portfolio?

➡ Can you create a portfolio that initially conveys the right message in between 5 to 15 seconds?

➡ Does the content you plan to include truly showcase your skills, experience, and creativity, as well as your best work?

➡ How will your portfolio as a whole help separate you from your competition in a positive way?

➡ Are you including the right amount of sample work, showing what you are capable of without overwhelming the client?

➡ Do you have testimonials or positive feedback from past clients that you can highlight?

Once you can answer these questions, you'll be in a better position to develop a portfolio that will help you generate new and additional business by impressing potential clients.

Tip #2: Be Relevant!

Once you choose a specialty for yourself and focus on a niche audience or specialized clientele, all of the work featured within your portfolio should be directly relevant to what the prospective client is looking for. For example, if you're a graphic designer who specializes in creating logos, business cards, and letterheads for companies, all of the samples in your portfolios should be examples of your best work in these categories. You may also be a talented illustrator or cartoonist, but that's not the type of work you're soliciting and probably not what your potential clients are looking for.

The trick to determining relevance is to really know who your target audience is and understand what it's looking for. As you choose content for your online portfolio, ask yourself, "Is this something I want my potential clients to see and base their evaluation of me on?"

Tip #3: Showcase the Right Amount of Work

The internet allows you to publish an unlimited amount of your work as part of your online portfolio. However, while your tendency may be to show off as much of your work as possible in hopes that something will appeal to the viewer, this is typically the wrong approach. Instead, focus on showcasing no more than a dozen samples of your work that truly highlight who you are, what you can do, and your specialty. If you're promoting yourself as having multiple specialties, showcase up to a dozen examples of each specialty but divide your portfolio into separate categories.

Tip #4: Add Your Bio

A short, well-written biography is the perfect complement to the samples of your work. A bio is not a resume. It's a summary of your background and accomplishments that's written in an informative and upbeat way. It can summarize your educational and work history, mention any awards or accolades you've earned, and succinctly summarize some of your more high-profile clients.

Within your bio, you can also talk about your philosophy of offering the best quality and most personalized service possible to your clients, how you have a history of working successfully under tight deadlines, and how you continuously use your past work experience and understanding of a particular industry, for example, to address the needs of your specialized clientele.

In just a few paragraphs, your bio should convey to the reader who you are, what your area of expertise is, and why you should be hired. It should also include a professional photograph of yourself. A photo adds a personal

---

CLICK TIP

To help showcase your professionalism and ability to cater to your clients, consider displaying testimonials from past clients on your website or as part of your online portfolio. You can solicit these testimonials, but make sure the clients give you permission to publish their words online. A handful of really positive testimonials can help boost your credibility, especially if you've worked with well-known companies. Keep the testimonials short and be sure they're properly credited. Anonymous testimonials are not useful and can be detrimental to your credibility because they're often not believable.

---

element to your bio and helps readers get to know you better by allowing them to put a face to the person they're reading about and whose work they're reviewing.

If you aren't a skilled writer, seriously consider hiring a freelance writer or public relations specialist to write your bio. The wording and tone you use in this document will impact how you're perceived by potential clients.

Tip #5: Invest the Time and Do Things Right

Even with the most powerful tools available to create an online portfolio, choosing the right samples of your work, formatting your portfolio, and properly customizing it to meet your goals is a time-consuming process. This is not something you can throw together in a few hours. Be sure you put a lot of thought and effort into the overall look and design of your portfolio, as well as into its content. Over time, fine-tune your portfolio so it evolves and always showcases your best and (if applicable) your most recent work.

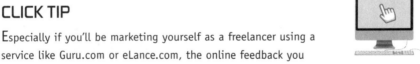

CLICK TIP

Especially if you'll be marketing yourself as a freelancer using a service like Guru.com or eLance.com, the online feedback you receive from clients is an essential sales tool in helping you land new clients, assuming the feedback you receive is 100 percent positive. Generating and accumulating a lot of positive feedback on these sites also allows you to charge more for your services and gives you a tremendous amount of extra credibility, which can help differentiate you from your competition.

Tip #6: Make Sure Your Portfolio Is Easy to Navigate

Not everyone is a skilled and experienced web surfer. Your online portfolio should be simple, to the point, and very straightforward in terms of its functionality. People should never have to question where they need to click next in order to see more of your work, contact you, or perform any other function your online portfolio offers.

> **WARNING**
>
> When someone is visiting your online portfolio, they should be easily able to find exactly what they're looking for with the bare minimum of keystrokes or mouse clicks. If people have to spend more than a few seconds looking for a specific sample of your work or your contact information, for example, they'll simply leave your site and surf elsewhere.

Adding various effects to your online portfolio are certainly possible. However, make sure these special effects don't distract the viewer or confuse them. Remember, the focus of an online portfolio is to showcase your best work, not entertain visitors with unrelated content.

If your online portfolio uses an onscreen menu or a series of navigation buttons, what each menu command or button actually does should be extremely obvious. They should also be easy to find and consistent on each page of your site. So, if the on-screen menu appears at the top of your portfolio's homepage, the same menu buttons should appear at the top of each subsequent page.

As you design your portfolio, think about what commands and functionality are truly important. Eliminate any extra options and choices that make your portfolio more complicated or confusing to explore. Keep it simple!

Tip #7: Keep Everything Professional

Everything within your portfolio should focus on presenting you as a highly professional and accomplished freelancer with a specific specialty or skill set. This is NOT the forum for conveying anything personal. It's not a personal blog or a Facebook or MySpace page used to communicate with friends and family. The people you want to be viewing your portfolio are potential employers. Thus, the content and tone of your online portfolio should reflect professionalism.

The content of your portfolio should present clear demonstrations of your work-related skills, experience, and accomplishments. If you're having trouble deciding whether specific content is relevant or appropriate, seek advice or a qualified second opinion.

Tip #8: Protect Your Work

Assuming the work showcased on your portfolio is original, make sure it's copyrighted and protect it using digital watermarks or other online protection schemes that disable a web browser's "Save As" or "Copy" feature, for example. The steps will prevent people from pirating your artwork or photographs, or using your materials without permission and without paying. Free online search engine services, like Yahoo! Images, automatically catalog artwork, photos, and digital images on websites and make it easy for people to copy this content or access it without permission if the content isn't properly protected.

Tip #9: Categorize Your Work

If you're a website designer who specializes in several different types of websites, bundle or display samples of similar work together so it's easier for potential clients to find and evaluate what interests them the most. If you're a graphic artist looking to design company logos for clients, for example, categorize and display the best samples of your logos together. Don't mix them in with examples of business cards, letterheads, brochures, signs, or illustrations. Properly categorizing your work helps establish your as a specialist and boosts your credibility quickly, especially if your portfolio showcases different types of work.

CLICK TIP

If a sample of your work requires an explanation in terms of what it was used for or how it helped a particular client achieve its goals, be sure to include a brief explanation in your portfolio. Don't keep people guessing. Tell people specifically what they're looking at and how your work was used to meet a client's needs or to solve a problem. Be succinct, but detailed in your explanations.

Tip #10: Pay Attention to Detail

Your portfolio must be 100 percent error free. This means that there should be no spelling or grammatical errors in the text, all captions should match their respective photos or images, and all links should work correctly. Visitors should be able to surf around your online portfolio using common sense to find exactly what they're looking for quickly and easily. Everything a visitor sees (or hears) when viewing your portfolio should help to communicate the overall message that you are a highly talented, creative freelancer who is able to perform the work the prospective client needs.

Use Your Portfolio to Set Yourself Apart from Your Competition

One additional consideration when developing your online portfolio is how you will set yourself apart from the competition. If someone views your portfolio and 10 or 20 others created by people with similar skills and experience, why should you be the person who gets hired? Somehow, your portfolio needs to address this question.

One potential problem you'll have dealing with competition is that if your online portfolio is available to the general public and not password protected, your competitors can easily check out your portfolio and your work, and then take steps to ensure their own website and/or portfolio is more impressive. Obviously, you can do the same thing by checking out your competition's online presence. One way to keep your competition guessing is to constantly update and fine-tune your online portfolio with new content.

You can also refrain from displaying your rates online. Encourage potential clients to contact you via e-mail or telephone to discover what you charge for your services. This makes it more difficult for your competition to undercut you from a price standpoint. Unfortunately, this approach creates one extra step for potential clients, who might not appreciate having to spend an extra few minutes contacting you to obtain the information and pricing they need.

Assuming you create an online portfolio that looks professional, it'll be the quality of your work and your credentials that set you apart from your competition, especially if you can effectively demonstrate expertise working in a specific field.

CLICK TIP

Be sure your online portfolio provides as much information about you as possible and that it answers the most common questions potential clients will have about your work. This will save them time in terms of getting their own questions answered and make their decision process that much easier. Your online presence should make it crystal clear about what types of services you provide. If a potential client feels the need to call you and ask "Can you do . . .," your online presence is not properly doing its job. Most importantly, make sure every page of your portfolio or website clearly displays your contact information—your name, address, phone number, cell phone number, and e-mail address.

Chapter 10

Marketing Yourself and Your Business in Cyberspace

$\mathcal{D}$eciding to launch your own business and work as an independent freelancer is a huge decision. The choice to create an online presence in order to market and sell your services to a worldwide audience is not just a prudent business choice, it also offers additional revenue-generating opportunities above and beyond working directly with local clients/customers in the real world.

Simply creating an online presence or e-commerce website isn't enough, however, to achieve your business goals, regardless of how professional, feature-filled, and impressive your website is. For the website to prove its usefulness, you'll need to develop ongoing ways to promote it and drive traffic (your target audience) to it. Traffic is essential for generating new business and fully utilizing your website as a promotional, sales, and business tool.

As you'll discover from this chapter and Chapter 11, there are numerous ways you can promote yourself, your website, and your freelance business both online and in the real world. There are no rules to follow or guaranteed formulas, however, that will drive traffic to your site. You'll need to develop and implement a personalized and ongoing marketing and promotional campaign that's customized to your own objectives. But there are some ways you can quickly and cost effectively market your business and your online presence. If done correctly, you'll start seeing results from your efforts within a few hours or days.

This chapter describes techniques for:

➡ Maximizing the effectiveness of your online portfolio to showcase your work

➡ Using online freelance match-up services, like Guru.com and eLance .com to generate new business

➡ Cross promoting your own website with other websites, including websites you've helped to create/design on behalf of current and past clients

➡ Taking advantage of search engine marketing and search engine optimization to drive qualified traffic to your website

➡ Using online display advertising

➡ Becoming actively involved with online social networking websites, like LinkedIn.com, MySpace.com, and Facebook.com to solicit new clients and customers and position yourself as an expert in your field

➡ Tapping the power of direct e-mail (but not spam) as a marketing tool

➡ Creating a blog, electronic newsletter, and/or podcast to share information, showcase your expertise, and attract new business

Depending on your goals and needs, it is not necessary to take advantage of each and every marketing or promotional idea described in this chapter and Chapter 11. Instead, based on your experience, knowledge, skills, creativity, budget, available resources, and goals, choose opportunities that you believe will generate the best results for what you're trying to accomplish. Ultimately, when it comes to marketing, you want to invest the least amount of time and effort to reach the largest number of potential customers/clients in your target audience. Thus, you want to track the results of your marketing, advertising, and promotional activities on an ongoing basis so that you can constantly fine-tune your efforts and improve results.

CLICK TIP

As a small, startup business trying to handle these objectives on your own, it's not at all realistic to expect the same results that a Fortune 500 company would generate with its multi-million dollar budget and with the services of an advertising agency and/or outside marketing firm.

As you move forward, it's important to understand that you can create and launch a comprehensive and effective marketing, advertising, and public relations campaign relatively quickly (within a week) but that it is an ongoing process. If your business is based on people visiting your website, it's essential that you constantly generate a steady flow of traffic to the site.

Because there is so much competition in cyberspace among established businesses and other freelancers, the marketing, advertising, and promotional efforts you implement need to be creative and separate you from your competition. It's your responsibility to pinpoint your target audience, develop a strong and high-impact marketing message, and then create ways to effectively communicate your message to potential customers/clients using the various resources at your disposal.

Your marketing, advertising, and public relations campaigns should all work together to achieve your business goals. Because each of these activities requires a unique skill set—one which professionals spend years perfecting—it might be a good business strategy to hire marketing, advertising, and public relations experts, at least initially, to help you create, launch, and manage your campaigns. Professionals help maximize your financial investment, avoid costly mistakes, and ensure that your efforts allow you to reach the perfect target audience with a marketing message that'll appeal to them. And if you can't afford to hire a company or other freelancers, or can only afford some services, read on.

Preparing Your Advertising, Public Relations, and Marketing Campaigns

The initial steps involved in creating and launching highly effective advertising, public relations, and marketing campaigns include covering the issues that define your business and your audience. They

➡ Create ads, press releases, marketing materials, and promotional items that effectively convey your message to its intended audience

➡ Calculate the overall budget you have at your disposal

➡ Figure out how much time you can invest in these efforts

Your next steps are to develop each facet of your campaign, prepare an appropriate timeline for launch, and determine how you'll accurately track the success of each element of your campaign so you can continuously fine-tune those efforts and use your budget more effectively. In other words, you need to know as quickly as possible what's working and what's not in terms of generating traffic to your site in a cost-effective manner.

There is no single solution or formula for creating the perfect comprehensive campaign to achieve your desired results. As you get to know your target customer and begin operating your business, you'll need to experiment a bit to determine which elements of your overall campaign are working well, which elements need to be fine-tuned, and which need to be scrapped and replaced with more cost-effective activities.

CLICK TIP

A multi-facetted approach is the best approach when it comes to advertising, marketing, and promoting your business. Don't rely on just one thing to drive traffic to your site. Ultimately, a steady flow of traffic to your website requires you to use many different promotional, marketing, and advertising activities simultaneously and on an ongoing basis. As you do this, expect that some activities will take time to have an impact. So make sure your expectations are realistic and that your budget is sufficient to sustain your efforts.

Freelance Matchup Services

As a freelancer, one way to easily find thousands of individuals and businesses looking to hire creative people with specialized skills for specific projects is to utilize one of the online-based freelancer match-up services, such as eLance.com or Guru.com. For the freelancer, these are fee-based services and you'll need to compete with many other freelancers to land jobs.

Your ability to generate business from these services depends on a variety of factors, including:

➡ Your ability to respond to available job listings posted on each site in a timely manner

➡ How customized and relevant your proposal is to the job you're bidding on

➡ How competitive your bid is for doing the work, compared to the competition

➡ How professional and relevant your portfolio is, based on the job offer you're responding to

➡ Your ability to meet the potential client's wants and needs, within his designated time frame and budget

WARNING

One problem with many online freelance services is that inexperienced freelancers bid on projects that they're not qualified to handle and their bids are for far less than fair market value for the work involved. Thus, an experienced freelancer who bids on the project based on what they're qualified to earn often gets underbid by someone offering to do the job for considerably less money. So while these services offer a great way for inexperienced freelancers to build up their portfolio, they are not necessarily a way for freelancers to earn top dollar for their hard work. When you start using a service like Guru.com or eLance.com, initially you'll need to bid very low to get work and build positive feedback. Once you've become established on the service and develop a positive reputation, you can bid higher for projects. See Chapter 14 for an in-depth interview with Inder Guglani, the CEO of Guru.com, where he offers valuable tips to freelancers on how to best use the Gutu.com service and services like it.

➡ The level of professionalism and customer service you convey within every e-mail or telephone conversation with a prospective client

➡ Your feedback, that is your rating that's posted on the service's website from past clients

The concept behind freelance match-up services is much like any employment website, only these offer additional services and functionality designed to help employers connect with qualified freelancers. Another difference is that it's the freelancers (not the employers) who pay to use the service, either in the form of a monthly fee or a fee per bid that they submit. Some of these services also charge the freelancer a commission, based on the amount of money earned from each project completed.

Because each service has a different fee structure, be sure you understand all of the fees involved with a service before signing up. Some of the popular freelance match-up services, which typically offer dozens of new job postings for web designers, graphic artists, photographers, and other creative professionals everyday, include:

➡ ContractedWork.com—contractedwork.com

➡ eLance.com—elance.com

➡ FreelanceDesigners.com—freelancedesigners.com

➡ GetAFreelancer.com—getafreelancer.com

➡ Guru.com—guru.com

➡ iFreelance.com—ifreelance.com

➡ MediaBistro.com—mediabistro.com

➡ Project4Hire.com—project4hire.com

➡ TalkFreelance.com—talkfreelance.com

➡ webDesignBids.com—webdesignbids.com/freelance_projects/web_site _designs.html

➡ webDesigners123.com—webdesigners123.com

Exchanging Website Links

Assuming the freelance work you do is impressive, one free and easy way to promote yourself and generate new business is to get your past and current clients to display a link on their websites that you helped to create that states, "web design by: [insert your name here]," "Graphic design work by: [insert your name here]," or "Photography by: [insert your name here]." Thus, as people visit your clients' websites, if they are impressed by your work, they can instantly link to your website and perhaps hire you. Meanwhile, part of your website should include a list of links to your past clients' websites, so your potential clients/customers can see additional samples of your work beyond what's displayed in your portfolio.

List Your Site with Search Engines

More than 80 percent of all web surfers use a search engine, such as Google or Yahoo! when they want to find something online. A tidbit of information, a particular website, or some type of specialized content is found using engines. There are literally hundreds of search engines and web directories available, but the most popular are Google and Yahoo!, then MSN.com, ASK.com, AOL Search.com, and AltaVista.com.

Your goal as an online business operator is first to get your website's URL listed with each of the major search engines, and then work toward optimizing your listing so it receives the best ranking and placement possible. After all, if you're in the graphic arts business and someone enters the search phrase "company logo design for pet stores," for example into Google, hundreds or

---

CLICK TIP

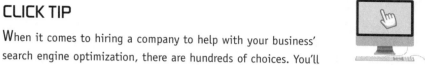

When it comes to hiring a company to help with your business' search engine optimization, there are hundreds of choices. You'll want to compare prices as well as services offered. Will the submission service simply get your website listed with the search engines, or will it take added steps to earn you excellent placement or a top ranking? Will the service evaluate your site to make sure its HTML programming will generate the best results with the search engines? Also, you'll need to determine if the service will keep your listing current on an ongoing basis, and whether this will cost extra.

---

thousands of relevant listings will probably show up. A typical web surfer will visit the first listing, and maybe the second and/or third for price comparison purposes. But, all subsequent listings will be ignored. This is why earning a top placement or ranking with each search engine is essential for driving traffic to your site.

The first step is to register your website with each of the major search engines. This can be done, one at a time, by manually visiting each search engine and completing a new website recommendation form. This process is time consuming and often confusing. An alternative is to pay a third-party submission service, such as Go Daddy.com's Traffic Blazer, to register your site with hundreds of the popular search engines simultaneously.

How to List Your Site with the Popular Search Engines

As soon as your website is published or posted on the web, you'll want to begin the process of listing it with the search engines and web directories. One way to speed up the process is to pay each popular search engine for premium placement, which is a topic covered later in this chapter. Why list your site with the search engines? Most web surfers begin their search for specific content from a search engine. They enter keywords or phrases, and then they follow the first few links provided by the search engine to reach the sites that might interest them. If someone is looking for the products or services you're selling and enters in a keyword that describes your offerings, by having your website listed with the search engines, that web surfer will be able to find you quickly and easily.

The search engines and web directories such as Yahoo! and Google are like telephone books where people can look up listings based on keywords or phrases. There are literally thousands of search engines and web directories on the internet, but the majority of web surfers tend to use the most popular search engines, so it's essential that your site be represented on these sites.

The cheapest way to get your site listed with the search engines is to visit each search engine yourself and complete the new listing submission form. The process is free and involves completing a brief questionnaire to help the search engine find and then catalog and categorize your proposed listing. It's important to understand that the listing submission process is different for each search engine and web directory, and that once you've completed the process, it will be necessary to update your listing periodically to maintain or improve your ranking or position.

When listing your site with some search engines and web directories, the process may be as simple as entering the URL address of your site and its title. The listing and submission process for other search engines, however, is much more in-depth and must be done correctly. In some cases, your site must be approved by a human before it gets listed.

> **CLICK TIP**
>
> While it's not necessary to get listed on every single search engine, your goal should be to obtain highly ranked listings on the most trafficked and popular search engines such as Yahoo! and Google in order to reach the most people.

The following links can be used to submit a listing for your new website on some of the most popular search engines and web directories:

- ➡ Google—google.com/addurl/
- ➡ Yahoo!—siteexplorer.search.yahoo.com/submit
- ➡ MSN Live Search—search.msn.com/docs/submit.aspx
- ➡ Ask—countrystarsonline.com/jimweaver/submit/askjeeves.htm
- ➡ AltaVista—altavista.com/addurl/default

A quicker, if more expensive way to get your site listed with the popular search engines, is to pay a third-party submission service to handle the process on your behalf. If you opt to use one of these services, be sure you understand exactly what you're paying for and what results you can realistically expect. For example, if you pay a service $39.95 to list your site on hundreds of the major search engines, chances are this will include a listing but will not guarantee prominent placement. To earn a high-ranking or prominent placement on a

> **CLICK TIP**
>
> A comprehensive introduction to search engine marketing and search engine submissions can be found at the Search Engine Watch website (searchenginewatch.com/showPage.html?page=webmasters).

search engine takes human intervention when submitting a listing with the search engines and when actually programming your website in order to provide exactly the information the search engines look for in the site's HTML programming and meta tags, for example. An inexpensive automated submission process does not typically guarantee a top-ranked listing.

Improving Your Site's Ranking and Position

After your site gets listed with a search engine and appears when searches are conducted by surfers, it then becomes your responsibility to keep your listing up to date and take whatever steps necessary to maintain and improve your listing. This is referred to as search engine optimization because your objective is to optimize the placement or ranking of a web surfer's search.

Again, this is a time-consuming process you can do yourself. You can also hire a SEO expert to handle it on your behalf, which will probably generate better results faster. If you want or need to have a listing for your site appear on the search engines quickly (as in within hours, not weeks), seriously consider using paid search engine marketing through Yahoo!, Microsoft, and/or Google AdWords to supplement your free listings. If you have a good-sized budget, you can also utilize display advertising and website sponsorships to ensure your message gets communicated to web surfers when they're online and actively looking for your company or its products.

Search Engine Optimization Tools and Resources

To find a third-party company that specializes in submitting URL listings to search engines as well as search engine optimization, enter the search phrase "search engine submissions" or "search engine optimization" into any search engine. You'll discover hundreds, potentially thousands, of paid services you can use, including:

➡ buildtraffic.com/indexnew.shtml
➡ engineseeker.com
➡ godaddy.com/gdshop/traffic_blazer/landing.asp
➡ iclimber.com
➡ networksolutions.com/online-marketing/index.jsp

- seop.com
- submitasite.com
- toprankresults.com
- trafficxs.com/platinum.htm
- worldsubmit.com
- wpromote.com/quicklist/landing/

CLICK TIP

Getting your online business listed with the popular search engines is one of the most cost-effective and powerful ways of driving qualified traffic to your website. This should be a priority when it comes to planning and then implementing your company's overall marketing, advertising, promotional, and public relations efforts.

Drive Targeted Traffic to Your Site Using Search Engine Marketing

It used to be that the most cost-effective, quickest, and easiest ways to drive traffic to your website was through online banner ads. These ads were purchased and appeared on websites that catered to the same demographic the advertiser was attempting to reach. However, as web surfers became more savvy, this changed. While display ads can still work and help build brand awareness, if your goal is to drive traffic to your website through the use of online advertising and marketing, search engine optimization and search engine marketing are currently the best ways to go, regardless of what you're selling.

Whenever you visit one of the popular search engines as well as many other types of websites, including blogs, you'll also notice short, text-based ads that are directly relevant to what you're searching for or to the content on the site you're currently visiting. These text-based ads are paid for by advertisers using one of several services, including:

- *Yahoo! Search Engine Marketing*—(866) 747-7327/sem.smallbusiness .yahoo.com/searchenginemarketing

➡ *Google AdWords*—adwords.google.com

➡ *Microsoft AdCenter*—advertising.microsoft.com/search-advertising

The main benefits of search engine marketing to the advertiser then, are:

➡ It's extremely inexpensive to launch a search engine marketing ad campaign. The initial investment is typically under $50 and you have 100 percent control over your daily ad spending. Once you set your budget, you pay only for the actual clicks to your site, not the impressions (people who see your ad).

➡ You can create and launch a fully customized search engine marketing campaign in just minutes and start seeing results within hours.

➡ The success of your campaign depends on your ability to select appropriate and relevant keywords that are being used by web surfers to find specific content on the web.

➡ You can track the success of your campaign in real time, using online-based tools provided by Yahoo!, Google, and/or Microsoft when you use their respective services.

➡ Your ad campaign can be expanded as you achieve success and generate a profit, or it can be modified or cancelled in minutes (not weeks or months) to address changes in your overall marketing campaign or your company's objectives.

Incorporating Meta Tags into Your Website's HTML Programming

In addition to accepting submissions from website operators, many search engines and web directories use automated "spiders" or "crawlers" to continuously search the entire World Wide web and gather details about new websites (and updates to existing sites) to list. How these automatic listings are gathered, cataloged, and categorized is based in large part on how your website utilizes *meta tags* and keywords throughout the site.

Meta tags are comprised of three parts: the title of your site, a description, and a list of keywords. The information you provide (by incorporating it into your site's HTML programming) is then used to categorize your site's content appropriately. In addition to the site's description, title, and a list of relevant keywords, within the HTML programming of your site, you'll need to incorporate a text-based, one-line *description* of your site, which again utilizes keywords to describe your site's content.

The more well thought out and comprehensive your meta tags are, the more traffic you'll ultimately drive to your site once it gets added to a search engine. If your website or e-commerce turnkey solution doesn't automatically incorporate meta tags into your website, there are many free online tools that allow you to create meta tags and appropriate HTML programming, and then cut-and-paste these lines of programming into your site with ease. No programming knowledge is actually required.

If you need help creating meta tags, use any search engine and enter the search phrase "meta tag creation," for example, or visit one of these websites:

- ➡ ineedhits.com/free-tools/free-metatags.aspx
- ➡ scrubtheweb.com/abs/builder.html
- ➡ anybrowser.com/MetaTagGenerator.html
- ➡ yooter.com/meta.php
- ➡ funender.com/phpBB2/meta_tag_creator.php

CLICK TIP

Meta tags can easily and quickly be incorporated into the HTML programming of any website. When you use a website or an e-commerce turnkey solution, this is often done on your behalf.

WARNING

When creating your keyword list for your site's meta tags and description, create a comprehensive list that's relevant to your site's content, but avoid excessive repetition of keywords and phrases. For example, don't use "logos, logos, logos, logos, logos." The search engine spiders identify repetition and hold this attempt at deception against you when cataloging and listing your site.

CLICK TIP

As the content of your website evolves and grows, be sure to update your meta tags to reflect this new and additional content. Keep in mind, it could take several weeks for your updates to be reflected with the individual search engines.

Launch Your Search Engine Marketing Ad Campaign

The first step to launching a search engine marketing campaign is to choose the service or services you'll use. Yahoo! Small Business' Search Engine Marketing, Google AdWords, or Microsoft AdCenter are the biggest. If you opt to use Google AdWords, for example, your ads will appear on Google whenever someone enters a search phrase that matches the keywords you select in your ad (providing you're willing to pay the going rate for that ad to be displayed, a concept that will be explained shortly).

In addition to Google AdWords ads being displayed through Google's own search engine site, the company has partnered with thousands of other websites and blog operators to display context-sensitive ads through the AdWords service. Google AdWords content network includes About.com, Lycos.com, FoodNetwork.com, The New York Times On The Web, InfoSpace, Business.com, HowStuffWorks.com, and literally thousands of other sites from around the world. According to Google, "The Google content network reaches 75 percent of unique internet users in more than 20 languages and over 100 countries. As a result, if you advertise on both the Google search network and the Google content network, you have the potential to reach three of every four unique internet users on Earth."

Yahoo! and Microsoft have similar content networks that allow targeted, text-based ads to be displayed on a wide range of websites well beyond each company's primary search engine or web directory. As you compare the search engine marketing programs you will want to compare rates and also determine if each respective company's content network will help you reach your company's own target audience.

Once you choose the company or companies you'd like to advertise with, the process of launching your campaign involves a few simple steps:

1. Set up an account with the search engine marketing company. This will require a credit card, debit card, or PayPal account to pay a deposit of about $50 to get started. (The deposit amount varies slightly.)

2. Create a detailed list of keywords that relate directly to the products/services your business offers. These keywords can include industry jargon, product names, your company's name, and any other words you deem relevant.

3. Create a text-based ad. Each ad should include a headline, a short body, and a URL that links directly to your website.

4. Decide on how much you'd like to spend on your campaign each day. Part of this decision includes deciding how much you're willing to pay each time someone sees your ad and clicks on it in order to reach your website. With this type of advertising, you do not pay for the number of impressions the ad receives. You only pay each time someone actually clicks on the link to visit your website. Based on the keywords you select, you'll be competing with other companies running ads with similar keywords. Using a complex formula that takes into account how much you're willing to pay-per-click, your ad(s) placement and the frequency it gets displayed will be determined. The more you are willing to pay-per-click, especially for popular keywords, the better your ad placement will be and the more frequently it will be viewed by

CLICK TIP

According to Yahoo!, as of July 2007, "Over 2.3 billion searches occur on Yahoo! each month. Prospective customers could be searching for what your business sells right now! Geographic targeting enables you to target your advertising to customers in your area or across the country." According to Microsoft, "We reach more than 465 million unique consumers each month globally, and 117 million in the United States."

web surfers actively using those same keywords to find what they're looking for online. Thus, when you launch your campaign, you must set a maximum cost-per-click, as well as your total daily spending limit, which can be as little as $10 per day.

5. As you create your search engine marketing campaign, you can also determine who will see your ad(s) based on geographic location.

6. To help you create a comprehensive and effective list of keywords, search engine marketing services offer a set of tools to assist you in creating your ad's keyword list and forecast how many impressions your ad will ultimately receive, based on your ad budget.

7. Once your ad campaign is running, you can use online tools to keep tabs on the number of overall impressions, click-thrus, ad placement, ad positioning, and related costs. This tracking is done in real time, so you'll know instantly if your campaign is working.

As you create your search engine marketing campaign, you'll come across a handful of advertising-related terms:

➡ *Click-Through-Rate (CTR)*. This refers to the number of clicks your website receives (as a result of someone clicking on an ad) divided by the total number of impressions (views) the ad received.

➡ *Cost-Per-Click (CPC)*. This number refers to the total cost of running the ad campaign, divided by the number of clicks to your site that you receive. The goal is for this number to be as low as possible. For example, if you pay $100 for a campaign that generates 10 hits, your CPC is $10 each. However, if that same $100 campaign generates 1,000 hits, your CPS is just $ .10 each.

➡ *Display URL*. This is the URL for your website that's actually displayed in your search engine marketing ad. In reality, you can have the ad link to any URL or any HTML page within your domain. If the Display URL is SampleSite.com, in reality, the link could lead a surfer to SampleSite.com/ProductInfo.htm.

➡ *Keyword*. This is a specific word or phrase that relates to a product, company, or any content on your website that you're advertising or promoting. When using search engine marketing, your text-based ad

---

ONLINE ADVERTISING TERMS

A complete glossary of terms can be found at Yahoo!'s website signup13.marketing solutions.yahoo.com/signupui/signup/glossary.do. Understanding these terms will help you better use the advertising tools that are at your disposal.

---

could be displayed when someone uses the search phrase that matches your keyword.

The Anatomy of a Search Engine Marketing Ad

Some of the reasons why text-based search engine marketing ads work so well are that the ads that appear for each web surfer are always directly relevant to the topic being searched. The ads are very short and to the point and they serve as links to websites that have the content the surfer is looking for at that very moment. From the advertiser's standpoint, this type of advertising can be extremely targeted by region and/or by keywords. Thus, these ads can quickly and efficiently prequalify potential customers/clients and attract them to your site at the precise moment they're looking for what your site offers.

In addition to ensuring your ads get the best possible placement on the search engine websites as well as throughout the appropriate websites within the search engine marketing company's content network, it's your responsibility as the advertiser to create a short, text-based ad that quickly captures the reader's attention and generates enough excitement for them to click on your link. Creating an effective search engine marketing ad takes creativity as well as a strong knowledge of your product and your target audience. What you say in your ad must be relevant, appealing, and attention getting. However, you have relatively little space to accomplish this task.

Regardless of whether you use Yahoo Search Engine Marketing, Google AdWords, Microsoft AdCenter, or another service, the anatomy of the ad that web surfers actually see will be basically the same. Every ad will have the following components:

➡ *Title.* This can be up to 40 characters long. It should be brief, but attention getting.

➡ *Description.* This portion of your ad can only be 70 characters long, so again brevity is essential, but what you say must make an impact and appeal directly to your target audience. When possible, incorporate one or more of your keywords into the ad itself (in both the title and the description). Two goals of your ad should be to announce that your online business offers the product or service the surfer is looking for, and then to somehow differentiate your online business from the competition, which may also be advertising using ads that surround yours on the surfer's screen. One way to do this is to offer some type of incentive for the potential customer/client.

➡ *Display URL.* This is the website address that will be displayed within the ad. The actual link, however, can lead to a different website, or a subpage within your domain. Ideally, the link should take the surfer directly to the product/service description page for what they're looking for rather than to your website's homepage. Don't make visitors responding to an ad have to search for what they want. When clicking the link in your ad, they should go right to that information.

From your perspective as the advertiser, it's easy to create and use a handful of ads that run simultaneously and incorporate different headlines and messages to appeal to slightly different target audiences. These ads then lead to the same place—your website. It's common for online business operators to run several different campaigns that use different content and different keywords simultaneously.

As you create your ads and each overall campaign, you need to create a list of relevant keywords that perfectly describe your product and/or your company. Who ultimately sees your ad depends heavily on the keywords associated with each ad. Ideally, the keywords you utilize should also correspond very closely to the content on your actual site. Each keyword can be a single word or a phrase that's up to 100 characters long. The web surfers who see your ad, however, don't actually see your keyword list.

The service you use will help you select appropriate keywords if you're having trouble compiling your list. Most of the services allow advertisers to associate up to 50 unique keywords or phrases with each of their ads. As you create your keyword list, you do not have to use multiple variations of a single word, such as "widget" and "widgets." Just make sure each word is spelled correctly.

Setting Your Search Engine Marketing Budget

One of the best things about search engine marketing campaigns is that they can be created and launched with a very low initial budget. You'll probably want to experiment with a few different ad variations and keyword lists until you create an ad that has a low cost-per-click and high click-through-rate. Once you've formulated one or more ads that generate appealing results, you should begin investing hundreds or thousands of dollars into that ad campaign. Spending thousands on a campaign that ultimately generates poor results wastes your money.

CLICK TIP

Services like Yahoo! Search Engine Marketing, Google AdWords, and Microsoft AdCenter all offer in-depth tutorials for new advertisers using their services. You'll also find a selection of tools designed to help you generate and monitor your ad campaigns. As an online business operator, make full use of these free services and tutorials to help you get the most out of every dollar spent on advertising. Ultimately, this will help increase your profits.

Online Display Advertising

Online display advertising allows you to purchase ad space on other websites that might appeal to your target audience. Your ads can use text, graphics, animation, sound, and even video to convey your marketing message. Unlike traditional print ads, however, someone who sees your online display ad can simply click on the ad and be transferred to your website in seconds in order to gather more information or make a purchase.

Running online display ads on popular websites costs significantly more than short, text-based search engine marketing ads. What your ad says and the visual elements used to convey the message (the overall look of the ad) are equally important. Thus, in addition to spending more to display your ads, you'll probably want to hire a professional advertising agency or graphic artist to design the ads themselves to ensure they look professional and are visually appealing, if you don't have the necessary skills.

Depending on where you want your online display ads to appear, the size requirements, ad content specifications, and how much you pay will vary dramatically. Besides choosing appropriate websites to advertise on, you'll need to select the exact placement of your ad on each website's page. Online real estate has value based on the potential number of people who will be seeing your ad and the physical size of your display ad (measured in pixels).

In general, the more people who will be seeing your ad, the higher the ad rates. Depending on the website, however, you may pay based on overall impressions (the number of people who simply see your ad) or how many people click on your ad. Another alternative is to pay a commission when a website offers a referral that results in a sale. The payment terms are typically created by the website on which you'll be advertising.

After creating a display ad that expertly conveys your message in a visually appealing way, your main objective as an advertiser is to find the perfect websites to advertise on. These should be sites that directly appeal to your target audience. You want your ad to be seen at precisely the moment someone wants to purchase the product you're offering. The best way to find these websites is to put yourself in your target customer's shoes and begin surfing the

---

WARNING

For someone with absolutely no advertising experience, it's extremely difficult to create professional-looking, effective ads and then know exactly where to have those ads run in order to generate the desired results. If you lack advertising experience, you could easily throw away a large part of your advertising budget by having poorly designed ads or by having well-designed ads appear in inappropriate online media.

---

web in search of sites that offer content that's appealing. Next, determine if those sites accept display advertising, and then request advertising information. Sites that accept display ads will typically have a link on the homepage that says "Advertise Here" or "Advertising Information."

Creating, launching, and managing a successful online display ad campaign requires specific skills. Instead of throwing away money on misguided advertising experiments, consider hiring an experienced advertising agency to help you, if online display advertising is going to be part of your overall advertising, marketing, public relations, and promotional efforts. You'll pay a bit more initially, but being able to use the experience and expertise of a trained advertising professional will ultimately generate much better results and higher sales.

Tapping the Power of Online Social Networking

Online social networking has become a way for people to meet in cyberspace, communicate, share ideas, and network. In addition to MySpace (myspace .com), Twitter (twitter.com), and Facebook (facebook.com), which are designed more for entertainment purposes, there are also online social networking services, such as LinkedIn (linkedin.com), that cater to business professionals. Developing an online presence on these sites and using the networking functionality offered can help you promote yourself as an expert in your field, find potential new clients, and promote your business.

Online social networking services are free to join. Your online profile can include your resume, contact information, and samples of your best work, and provide a forum for you to subtly promote your marketing message. Keep in mind, however, that social online networking services do not allow members to blatantly advertise their businesses (unless you pay for advertising on the service), so don't harass your online contacts (friends) with spam messages, bulletins, or

CLICK TIP

In addition to joining and becoming active on the more mainstream social networking websites, look for a services that cater more to the industries or interests that you specialize in working with or that comprise your target audience.

other communications that can be construed as blatant advertising, as opposed to a more subtle exchange of information and ideas, which is what these services were designed to promote.

Permission-Based (Opt-In) E-Mail Marketing

Permission-based marketing is a term used to describe asking for and securing permission from your customers, clients, and website visitors to send them information via e-mail. Providing they agree, you can send information ranging from simple e-special offers to elaborate e-newsletters and e-catalogs, depending on your marketing objectives.

Regardless of the information you send, gaining permission brings three benefits. First, if people ask to be included in your electronic mailings, in all likelihood they have an interest in the products and services you're offering. Second, by securing permission, you won't be spamming—that is, sending e-mail messages without the recipient's permission. Third, you will be building a very valuable in-house mailing list, which can be used for any number of research and marketing purposes. On that note, you will need to purchase customer database software so you can compile, store, and manage your subscriber base.

PURCHASE A MAILING LIST THAT TARGETS YOUR EXACT CUSTOMERS

You can purchase e-mail mailing lists of businesses that might be interested in hiring you on a freelance basis. For example, if your specialty is designing websites for dentists, you could purchase or license an e-mail list of dentists. Harris Info Source (rapidreachonline.com/lp/rapid_reach_email_marketing.html), Wholesale Mailing Lists (wholesalemailinglists.com), List Solutions (listsolutions.com), and InfoUSA (infousa.com) are examples of companies that license or sell targeted and highly customized e-mail mailing lists.

Creating a Blog, Electronic Newsletter, or Podcast to Promote Your Business

One way to demonstrate and share your knowledge and expertise while at the same time, promoting yourself as an expert in your field and your availability as a freelance creative professional is to create and distribute a blog, vlog, online newsletter, podcast, or videocast on a regular basis. (Video content can be distributed through services like YouTube or iTunes, for example.) By offering potential customers free information they perceive to be valuable, they're more apt to read, watch, or listen to your blog, newsletter, podcast, or videocast. And they'll be more receptive to the marketing message incorporated in this free content.

It's essential, however, that the content you create and distribute be professional, informative, easy-to-access, and free. It should also showcase samples of your best work and promote you as a highly skilled, knowledge-able, and experienced freelancer capable of meeting the needs of potential clients. Within the content you distribute can be informative how-to articles, testimonials, samples of your work, answers to common questions clients

CLICK TIP

To learn more about podcasting and how to get started using podcasting as a marketing tool for your business, visit any of these websites: en.wikipedia.org/wiki/Podcasting, bswusa.com/podcast.asp, podcast.net, podcasting-tools.com, or podcastingnews.com/articles/What_is_Podcasting.html.

WARNING

Before investing vast amounts of money on any campaign, do your research, make projections, forecast response rates and potential profits, and whenever possible, test out each element of your campaign before doing a full-scale launch. As you'll discover, many considerations and decisions go into creating, launching, and managing an overall advertising, marketing, and promotional campaign. The more time you invest developing your skills in these areas, doing your research, and then analyzing your results, the better off you'll be ultimately.

have, third-party reviews of your work, information about industry trends, advice for potential clients, and/or summaries of relevant research your potential clients and customers would be interested in.

Chapter 11

Marketing Yourself and Your Business in the Real World

*I*f you learn nothing else from this book, take away this essential piece of wisdom: If you build it, they won't come. That is, unless you invest the time, effort, and money necessary to properly promote your business venture and continuously drive traffic to your site. Simply publishing your website on the internet is not enough. If people don't know about your site, the chances of them simply stumbling upon it are slim. Sure, getting listed on the internet search engines is extremely important, but it could take weeks or even months for your site to get listed and even longer to earn a good ranking, unless you pay a premium to get listed.

When it comes to promoting, marketing, and advertising your business, you have a wide range of opportunities, both in the real world and in cyber-space. Based on what you'll be selling and to whom you'll be selling, you'll probably want to take a multifaceted approach to generate as much traffic to your site as possible in order to have new customers and clients. And as you already know, simply driving traffic to your website isn't enough either. Once someone visits your site, it must contain the content and information neces-sary to transform that visitor into a buyer or paying customer/client.

Every business, regardless of what products or services it offers, needs to be marketed, promoted, and advertised to its target audience. These activities overlap somewhat and should all be done in a way that communicates the same overall message to your intended audience.

For the purposes of this book, marketing relates to attracting customers through word of mouth or participating in community/charitable events, for example. Sponsoring a Little League team in your community (and getting your logo displayed on the team's uniforms), is an example of a grassroots, localized marketing approach. Public relation activities that require you to use the media in order to obtain free editorial coverage in newspapers, maga-zines, newsletters, on websites, television, and the radio, would fall under your company's marketing efforts.

Promotion involves spreading the word about your company through special sales (buy one, get one free, or 30 percent off your first purchase), which encourage potential customers to try out your product/service. A pro-motional activity might include giving out free items, like pens, with your company's name, logo, or contact information, or having a booth at a trade show.

Advertising is paying to have your message appear in magazines, on radio, in newspapers, on television, on billboards, or in any other media outlet. When you pay for advertising, you have 100 percent control over the message and its placement. You determine exactly what, where, and when people see or hear, based on the advertising media you utilize.

Depending on a variety of factors, including what services you'll be offering, what you'll be selling, your target audience, your budget, the amount of time you have to invest, your desired goals, and your creativity, there are a number of ways you can get the word out about your business in the real world, including:

➡ paid advertising in newspapers, magazines, and newsletters, on radio and television, and in other forms of traditional media, including industry-oriented or special interest publications.

➡ a public relations effort designed to get the media to feature information about you (as an expert in your field), your business, and your products in articles, product reviews, feature stories, and news stories.

➡ innovative promotions designed to appeal directly to your target audience, such as cross-promoting your business with other businesses, sponsoring events, and coming up with unique ways of interacting with your potential customers/clients in order to inform them about your online business and its products.

➡ marketing materials that promote your website and your core message, including printed catalogs, fliers, newsletters, bumper stickers, promotional T-shirts, or other giveaways with your company's name, URL, logo, and/or message imprinted on them that you distribute at trade shows, conventions, special events, and other gatherings attended by people in your target audience.

CLICK TIP

Depending on what you're selling and the services you'll be offering, as well as your budget and your target audience, you might wish to incorporate other well-established marketing, advertising, or promotional activities into your efforts. This might include launching a telemarketing campaign, cold calling potential customers, or sponsoring some type of event that's of interest to your target audience.

➡ positive word-of-mouth and referrals from existing customers, best achieved by offering the absolute best customer service possible, developing a positive and ongoing relationship with all of your customers, and selling only top-quality products.

Again, the very best approach when it comes to advertising, marketing, and promoting your business is multifaceted; that is, not relying on just one thing to drive traffic to your site and generate business. For example, don't just purchase a bunch of advertising space in one magazine or newspaper and expect that hundreds of potential clients will see your ad, visit your site, and become paying customers. Likewise, don't just send out one press release to a bunch of media outlets and expect that your company and its products/services will receive national coverage in newspapers, magazines, on radio, and on television.

Ultimately, driving a steady flow of traffic to your website requires you to use many different promotional, marketing, and advertising activities simultaneously and on an ongoing basis. As an individual handling these tasks on your own, it's not realistic to expect the same results that a Fortune 500 company or an established agency would generate with its multimillion dollar budget and the services of an advertising agency and/or outside marketing firm. But you can get results.

Anyone can learn how to effectively market, promote, and advertise her own business, services, and products. Just plan on experiencing a learning curve as you try different approaches to determine what works best when it comes to reaching your target audience in the most cost-effective, efficient way possible.

Preparing Your Advertising, Public Relations, and Marketing Campaign

The initial steps involved with creating and launching a highly effective advertising, public relations, and marketing campaign include:

➡ Learning everything there is to know about the products/services you'll be selling.
   · your key selling points

- why your offerings will appeal to customers
- what problems you can help to solve
- how you can make the life of your customer/client easier or better
- the perceived value of what you're offering to the customer
- what sets your business apart from the competition

➡ Determining exactly what the message is you're trying to convey.

➡ Pinpointing the exact target audience you're trying to reach.

➡ Creating ads, press releases, marketing materials, and promotional items that effectively convey your message to its intended audience.

➡ Calculating the overall budget you have at your disposal.

➡ Figuring out how much time you can invest in these efforts.

➡ Soliciting the assistance of experienced experts.

Your next steps are to develop each facet of your overall advertising, marketing, and promotional campaign; prepare an appropriate timeline for launch; and determine how you'll accurately track the success of each element of your campaign so you can continuously fine-tune those efforts and use your budget more effectively. In other words, as quickly as possible, you need to know what's working and what's not in terms of generating traffic to your site in a cost-effective manner.

PLAN YOUR REAL WORLD ADVERTISING IN ADVANCE

Depending on the type of advertising, marketing, public relations, and promotions you do, you may be able to track the success of each component of your overall campaign starting immediately. It may, however, take several weeks or even months for you to be able to determine if a specific aspect of your campaign was successful. Many media outlets work on a *lead time*. For a monthly magazine, issues are created well in advance. So, if you'd like to advertise in the November issue (or use your public relations efforts to have a product review appear in that issue), you'll need to get everything set up months in advance.

You'll quickly discover that there is no single solution or formula for creating the perfect comprehensive campaign that will achieve your desired results. As you get to know your target customer and begin operating your business, you'll need to experiment a bit to determine which elements of your overall campaign are working well, which elements need to be fine-tuned, and which need to be scrapped and replaced with more efficient or cost-effective activities.

During this process, learn as much as you can about advertising, marketing, and public relations fundamentals. You can do this by reading books, taking classes, or hiring experts and learning from them. You can also carefully evaluate what your competition is doing, see what works for them, and try to emulate those activities after properly customizing them to meet your needs.

Advertising Your Site

In terms of your overall marketing mix, *advertising* involves paying to have the marketing message you create—your advertisement—aired on radio or television, and/or printed in newspapers, magazines and other publications, or displayed online. By paying the media to run your ad or display it, you're given 100 percent control over its content. Depending on the media, this includes what it says, what it looks like, how it sounds, its size or its length, and when it's seen or heard.

Advertising certainly has its advantages in terms of being able to reach your target audience with your very specific message. However, depending on where you advertise, it can also be costly. As a general rule, for paid advertising to really work, it requires frequency. Thus, your intended audience must see or hear your ad multiple times before you can expect it to respond by visiting your website. Running one single, 60-second radio ad or one print ad in an industry-oriented newspaper or magazine, for example, probably won't generate an overwhelming response.

For paid advertising to work and for you to get the most out of it based on the amount of money being spent, you must be able to reach your target audience with the right message. This requires you to brainstorm the right wording to use, the appearance of your ad (in print), or how it will sound (on radio), for example. The ad you create is often referred to as the "creative" in the advertising industry—whether it's a print ad or a television or radio spot. The ad you create should have a well-defined goal, such as introducing your intended audience to your product/service, or driving people to your website.

Once you've written and produced what you believe to be the perfect ad, the next step is to secure proper placement in the media. This refers to when and where it will appear and how often. When you purchase advertising space or time, it's referred to as a "media buy." Your media buy should be with media outlets—newspapers, magazines, newsletters, radio stations, television stations, websites, or other media outlets—that allow you to reach your target audience.

Part of being a successful advertiser involves finding media outlets that you can afford and that will allow you to reach your target audience as effectively as possible. Typically, when you're paying for advertising, the more advertising space or time you purchase, the more of a discount you're given. The advertising rates you pay are often highly negotiable.

Start by pinpointing what media outlets you'd benefit from advertising in. Next, determine the cost associated with creating the ad you wish to run. You'll then need to contact each appropriate media outlet's advertising department and request a media kit. This kit will include advertising rates and ad specifications, plus information about the media out-

> **CLICK TIP**
>
> As a freelance website designer, graphic artist, or photographer looking for new clients, consider advertising in industry-oriented publications that target individuals or companies in specific industries that might have a need for your services.

let that potential advertisers can use to decide whether or not to advertise. Based on the price list and information within the media kit, you can determine if running your ad with that specific media outlet is affordable and conducive to achieving your desired results.

If your business will be selling a very specialized or niche product or service to a specific audience, you'll want to find special interest or industry-oriented publications that cater to that audience. While running an ad in a

CLICK TIP

When you run an ad, you want to determine how many people overall will be exposed to it, that is, the number of "impressions" your ad will make. From that number, you then want to determine how many responses you receive. For example, how many people saw or heard your ad and immediately visited your website. Another important statistic to track is how many people who visited your site purchased your products/services. Ultimately, the orders generated are what increase your business' revenues. Paying for ads that don't generate enough sales or a high enough response rate is pointless.

general interest magazine such as *Time, Newsweek, Us Weekly,* or *People* will allow you to reach millions of readers, how many of those people actually fit into your target demographic? If it's only 5 or 10 percent of the readers, spending tens of thousands of dollars (or more) to run that ad in a general interest magazine is pointless, because you're paying to reach too many people whom you already know have no interest in what you're selling.

Instead, it would make more sense to find a special interest publication that may only have a circulation of 5,000 at least 80 to 90 percent of the readers are part of your target audience.

Pinpointing the best media outlets to advertise with, whether it's within print (newspapers, magazines, or newsletters), on electronic (radio or television), or online (websites or search engines), will play a tremendous role in your success and determine what type of response you receive from the ad.

In addition to creating the perfect ad and then selecting the most appropriate media to showcase your ad, another challenge all advertisers face is making their ad stand out from all the others. As consumers, we've become trained to tune out advertising. As an advertiser, however, your goal is to create an ad (or series of ads) that captures people's attention. Accomplishing this requires creativity.

If you read any newspaper as a consumer, how many ads do you actually take more than a few seconds to glance at? What about the ads in the magazines you read? How much time do you spend glancing at each of them before turning the page? Typically, it's only a few brief seconds. As the advertiser, your goal must be to capture the reader's attention in that brief time, and not get totally lost among all the other ads.

If you're advertising on radio or television, you only have that same few seconds to capture listener's attention before they switch stations, walk way from their television for a snack, or engage in some other activity that distracts them until their programming returns. With so many things to consider when creating and executing an advertising campaign, make sure your initial expectations are realistic. Expect to make some mistakes early on and be prepared to fine-tune your campaign until the ad message and the ad placement is right, based on what you're selling and to whom you're selling it.

CLICK TIP

When selecting media outlets, focus on reaching your target audience in a cost-effective way. Figure out how you can spend the least amount of money to reach the largest number of people in your target audience. This often involves advertising in a handful of different media outlets and using several different advertising mediums. Because you're paying to place your ads and you have total control over the content, it's essential that your ads communicate the most compelling message possible, as quickly as possible, in order to generate the best response rate.

Public Relations 101

Public relations efforts involve working with the same media outlets you'd advertise with, but in a very different way. Using public relations strategies, your goal is to work with reporters, writers, editors, and journalists to convince them to include information about you, your company, and your products in their editorial content.

This might mean getting interviewed as an expert in your field as part of a relevant a news story, having your product featured in a review, or having your products/services somehow included in news, features, or human interest

CLICK TIP

To learn how to write and format a press release, visit one of these websites: publicityinsider.com/release.asp, press-release-writing.com/10_essential_tips.htm, internetbasedmoms.com/press-releases/; or wikihow.com/Write-a-Press-Release.

stories that make up the editorial content of newspapers, magazines, radio shows, and television talk shows (and news programs).

When you use public relations, you provide reporters, writers, editors, and journalists with the information they need for their articles or stories. However, you have absolutely no control over what's written or said. You run the risk that details about your message will be misrepresented or that important details will be left out.

The benefit to public relations, however, is that when you, your company, and/or your products or services are featured in various media outlets, you don't pay a penny. And when readers, listeners, or viewers read or hear about your product/service from a reporter or journalist they trust, they're more apt to buy the product, or at least visit your website to learn more about it than those who simply read or hear an ad.

The trick to generating positive publicity is to develop relationships with writers and editors who currently reach your target audience. This relationship can be established initially by sending a detailed press kit or press releases about your company and its products/services, and, if applicable, a sample of the product for the reporters, writers, editors, and journalists to review firsthand.

Every day, the media is literally bombarded with dozens, sometimes hundreds, of press releases and press kits. Thus, the information you provide must adhere to a specific format, be comprehensive, be of interest to the journalist, and be timely. You must also take into account the lead time of reporters and be conscious of their often tight deadlines.

The easier you make it for media representatives to include information about you, your company, and/or your product(s) in their articles, features, reviews, or segments, for example, the better your chances are of receiving the free coverage you're seeking.

As in advertising, planning and executing an effective public relations campaign takes skill, creativity, experience, and the ability to capture the attention of the media in a positive way. If done correctly, being featured in a single newspaper or magazine article, or on a radio or television program, can easily generate a better response than spending tens of thousands of dollars on paid advertising. Once the publicity appears in the media, you'll see immediate results in the form of additional traffic to your site.

The best way to generate free publicity is to write a well-written press release about your company and/or products/services. This press release must adhere to a standard press release format, contain a newsworthy message, be well-written, and contain all of the information reporters need. Answer the questions who, what, where, when, why, and how. A typical press release is double-spaced and fits on one or two pages.

CLICK TIP

In addition to having copies of your press materials that can be mailed to targeted reporters, writers, editors, and journalists, you'll also want to create a "Press," "Press Room," or "Media" area on your website that contains these materials and makes them available for downloading by members of the media.

A press kit is a folder that contains press releases, details about your product, along with a one- or two-page company background, short biographies of company executives, product photos, and copies of press clippings already generated about the company.

If you've never written a press release or press kit, consider hiring a freelance public relations specialist or a PR firm to assist you with the process. Being able to determine exactly what information a member of the media wants or needs, and presenting that information to them properly is essential.

After your press materials are created, the next step is to compile a list of specific recipients, based on their "beats"—the topics they typically report on or write about. This is your customized media list.

There are several ways to track down the right people to send your press materials to at various media outlets, but first, you need to create a list of media outlets you want to target in hopes of generating publicity. Next, contact each media outlet and obtain the name, title, address, phone number, and e-mail address for the appropriate person at that media outlet. An alternative is to purchase a comprehensive media directory that lists this information.

Bacon's Media Directories (866-639-5087/us.cision.com/products_services /bacons_media_directories_2008.asp) provide a comprehensive listing of all

> ## CLICK TIP
>
> By positioning yourself as an expert in your field, you could be invited to be interviewed by the news media as part of a timely news story that relates to your area of expertise. Or, you could be invited to be a guest on a talk radio show or television talk show. As a guest, you can plug your products/services and direct people to your website while building credibility with the audience at the same time.

newspapers, magazines, radio stations, and television stations, along with contacts at each media outlet. The printed directories are updated annually, and a complete media database is also available online for a fee.

Several other companies offer similar directories and databases. The reference section of a public library may be a good resource for this information. These directories include:

- ➡ The Gebbie Press All-In-One Media Directory—gebbie.com/(845) 255-7560
- ➡ Media Contacts Pro—mediacontactspro.com/products.php/(800) 351-1383
- ➡ Burrelles/Luce—burrellsluce.com/MediaContacts/(800) 368-8070

To save money compiling your media list, consider visiting a large newsstand, looking through all of the newspapers and magazines, and then checking the masthead of each appropriate publication for the proper contact details. You can also review the ending credits of television talk shows and news programs, and contact news and talk radio stations.

Mastering the art of working with the media to generate free publicity can be an extremely cost-effective way to promote your business and build its positive reputation on a local, regional, national, or even international level, especially for those on a shoestring budget.

Public relations can be an extremely powerful tool if used correctly, and should definitely be a prominent part of your overall marketing/advertising campaign for your business. You'll find that once you start

---

CLICK TIP

Once your press release is written, to save time and potentially money, you can pay a press release distribution service such as PR Newswire (prnewswire.com) to distribute it electronically, via fax, or by U.S. mail to the media outlets or media contacts you desire. Within hours, thousands of reporters, writers, editors, and journalists could have information about you, your company, and your products waiting within their in-box.

---

generating positive publicity, that other media outlets will eventually start coming to you in order to feature you, your company, or your products within their editorial coverage.

Marketing Strategies

Marketing for your business can mean many different things and encompass a wide range of activities—from adopting top-notch customer service practices within your organization to ensure your customers will provide positive word-of-mouth advertising for your products to sponsoring a Little League team in your city and having your company's name and website URL displayed on the players' uniforms.

One time-tested marketing strategy involves having your logo, website URL, and marketing message imprinted on giveaway items such as T-shirts, hats, buttons, pens, or bumper stickers, and then distributing the giveaways to potential customers. This can be done at special events, at trade shows or conventions, or by mailing them to current and potential customers.

As with any type of advertising, public relations, promotional activity, or marketing, what you opt to do should be cost-effective, target your audience, and allow you to communicate your marketing message in a way that's suitable for what you're selling and to whom you're selling.

Chapter 12

Interacting With and Managing Clients

*L*aunching your online business and marketing generates interest in your products or services. However, the next steps involve transforming potential clients/customers into paying ones, and then building long-term relationships in order to generate repeat business and positive word-of-mouth referrals. To accomplish this, absolutely nothing replaces the need to provide top-notch customer service to each and every one of your clients/customers, 100 percent of the time.

CLICK TIP

The information in this chapter pertains to freelancers who will be soliciting business using the internet and their website. It does not apply to people adopting an e-commerce-based business model. The approach you'd take to promote yourself online is different from creating an online presence (e-commerce website) designed to actually sell products/services and accept orders via the web.

If you're operating an online-based venture, even if your business model involves minimal direct (in-person or telephone) interaction with your clients/customers, it's still essential that your website promote a well-thought-out and elaborate customer service strategy to ensure customers always experience the most positive experience possible when doing business with you. Making yourself available via telephone and/or e-mail for your clients/customers is essential for building confidence in your business. People need to feel that they can get their questions answered and their concerns addressed in a timely and highly personalized way.

If your business model involves interacting with your customers and clients on a more personalized (in-person) level in order to do custom work for them, offering a superior customer service experience is essential for differentiating yourself from the competition.

It's one thing to simply meet your professional obligations and the expectations of a customer by finishing your work on time and correctly. This is the absolute bare minimum of what's required of you as an independent freelancer. It's another thing altogether to surpass expectations, personally address all concerns and questions, meet all deadlines, and provide top-quality and highly professional work that's completed within budget. To help create the most positive experience for your clients, providing additional value-added services that go above and beyond what's expected, and conveying a positive, friendly, and up-beat attitude, while also doing anything and everything to properly address the needs and wants of your clientele, are what properly managing your customers and clients is all about.

Even the smallest of gestures, such as sending a thank-you note for an order, or making a follow-up phone call to ensure your products/services are meeting or exceeding the expectations of your clients, will help to set you apart from your competition and build up strong and long-term relationships with your clients. As you develop your strategies and plans for how you'll conduct your business, focus on providing the highest and friendliest level of customer service possible during every single interaction you have with your clientele, whether that interaction is online, on the telephone, in person, or via written correspondence. It takes a long time and hard work to build a strong and positive reputation for yourself and your business, but it only takes one or two small mistakes to destroy that reputation, lose business, and hurt your chances of long-term success as a freelancer and/or online business operator.

Being able to provide the highest level of customer service—both online and in the real world—means truly understanding the wants and needs of your customers and then always addressing them. It also means having the energy and insight to build a relationship with each and every client in order to generate repeat business and referrals. You'll discover that no matter what business model you're following, it's always easier and cheaper to generate business from people you've successfully worked with in the past than it is to constantly have to seek out and generate new customers and clients.

SUCCESS REQUIRES SACRIFICE

As a business operator, your goal is to earn high profits yet work as little as possible. However, you have to develop an equitable balance between your own needs and those of your clients. Failure to provide your customers/clients with the attention they want, need, and deserve will result in their unhappiness and frustration. Unhappy clientele ultimately means more work for you, less revenue, and a more difficult time generating new business. As a freelancer, expect to work hard and make personal sacrifices for your clients in order to truly be competitive in today's marketplace.

Also, over the long term, it is a much more cost-effective use of your time and resources to go out of your way to provide the highest quality of service upfront, as opposed to having to deal with customer complaints or address problems or miscommunications down the road.

This chapter focuses on how to properly manage your customers and clients and build long-term relationships with them. It offers tips for generating positive word-of-mouth referral business over the long term. Remember, at the core of every good business relationship, no matter what product or service you're offering (in the real world or online), is offering the highest level of customer service possible.

Determining Exactly What the Job Entails

Developing a strong, long-term relationship with clients begins at the very first interaction. As a freelancer, it's your job to sell your skills, experience, knowledge, and abilities to clients in a way that appeals to them and addresses their wants and needs. Thus, the first step in developing a relationship is to listen! Listen carefully to what each prospective client/customer has to say about his wants, needs, and concerns. Learn as much as you can about the prospective client, and cater your sales pitch/proposal specifically to him. If a prospective client believes you truly understand him, have the ability to meet his needs, and demonstrate a hard working, friendly, and positive attitude, you'll be well on your way to landing new business.

As soon as a prospective client shows any interest whatsoever in hiring you, take steps to determine his specific wants and needs, while at the same

---

WARNING

Never offer a quote for a freelance job until you truly understand what the job entails, the client's expectations, and his deadline and budget. Then, as you prepare your proposal and price quote (or bid), make sure you'll be able to live up to whatever you promise, without compromising the quality of your work, having to increase your fees, or missing an important deadline.

time figuring out what his expectations are in terms of the relationship he's hoping to build. Develop an understanding of his goals while also figuring out his timeline and budget. Ask plenty of questions, so you can address his unique challenges, concerns, and questions. The more information you gather early on about your prospective client, the easier it will be for you to cater your products and services to him effectively and efficiently.

Right from the start, keep detailed notes of your conversation(s) with prospective clients. When it comes time to creating your contract or written agreement, absolutely everything pertaining to the project should be outlined, so both parties are on the same page, have realistic expectations, and understand how the process will work moving forward.

Also, you want to list specifically what is included in your quote/proposal and what isn't, so if down the road additional work is required above and beyond what was initially discussed and agreed to, the client will understand additional fees will be charged. Likewise, if the quality of your work isn't up to par or for whatever reason it does not meet the requirements spelled out in your agreement, it will be your responsibility to redo the work until it meets the client's needs. In this scenario, any extra work you need to put it will be at your own expense. Only by listening carefully to what your client has to say initially and by asking specific questions will you be able to develop a thorough understanding of what a job entails before you actually begin calculating your quote or doing the work.

Negotiating Prices and Deadlines

When it comes to website design, for example, how long it takes for a freelancer to complete a project varies greatly from person to person, based on skill, experience, knowledge, and other variables. Thus, a specific project might take one freelancer 10 hours to complete, while it will take another freelancer with similar skills 15 to 20 hours to complete.

As a freelancer, it's essential that you understand how you work and how quickly you can accomplish various tasks. Once you comprehend what's involved with a specific project, you'll be able to make educated calculations about how long a project will take you to complete. Knowing this, you can formulate an accurate and fair price quote or bid.

It's often easier for freelancers to charge a flat fee on a per-project basis rather than an hourly rate. This helps the client accurately calculate costs and allows you to perform your best work without having to worry about billing for too many hours (compared to what your competition would bill for a similar project).

Figuring out how much to charge for a project is always a challenge for a freelancer. While you want to earn fair market value for your work, based on your background experience, you also want your bids to be competitive compared to your competition. There are always competitors, both domestically and overseas, who will undercut you on price, regardless of how low your prices are. Thus, it is your responsibility to justify your pricing based on the quality of your work. In other words, as a freelancer, it's necessary to let your work speak for itself when it comes to demonstrating to prospective customers/clients that you're well worth what you charge.

Customers and clients often pay a premium to ensure top-quality results for the custom work they commission, and don't mind paying for superior customer service and reliability. As you set your pricing or create bids for specific projects, keep in mind that your prospective customers and clients will evaluate your pricing based on the following criteria:

- Bids from your competitors
- The quality of your work (your portfolio)
- Your professional reputation
- Your ability to complete the project on time
- The quality of customer service and level of professionalism you exhibit
- Your feedback/ratings from past clients

Given your workload, make sure you have the ability to generate the desired results on time and within budget before taking on any project. Failure to do this is unprofessional and results in an unhappy client. Make sure you and your customer/client agree in advance on deadlines (and put them in writing).

By communicating openly with your client in advance, outlining the entire project, and then developing a detailed timeline for completing it, you'll help ensure the client remains confident in your abilities and happy

SET A TIMETABLE WITH YOUR CLIENTS

If you're working with a client for the first time, create and agree to a series of mini-deadlines, or milestones, for completing the project. For each milestone, determine what percentage of the overall project should be completed, such as 25, 50, 75, and 100 percent, and then set a deadline for each. When you reach each milestone, communicate with the client and share your progress, while at the same time soliciting feedback. This ensures that you and the client are on the same page and maintain the same overall vision. It also helps eliminate any misunderstandings that could require you to redo work or perform additional work beyond what was agreed to in order to make the client happy after the project is complete. This communication with your client can be done via e-mail, by phone, or in person.

with your overall work and performance as a freelancer. Use the worksheet in Figure 12.1 to help you develop specific milestones for each project leading up to its completion.

As you develop a relationship with each new client and begin discussing the project you'll be working on, make sure you're dealing primarily with a decision maker who is authorized to approve your proposal or bid and who has the authority to set deadlines for the project, review your work, and provide feedback on behalf of the client. Your goal should be to gather enough information early on so that you can create a competitive profile and bid that clearly sets you and your work apart from the competition in a positive way. The more customization you do in your proposal to address the client's specific needs, goals, concerns, and plans, the better your chances will be of getting hired, especially if what you're ultimately offering are solutions.

Many freelancers have an hourly rate for their time, one that takes into account operating expenses and their overall costs of doing business. If you'll be bidding on a project based on a flat fee, consider how much time the project will realistically take you to complete, and then develop your bid taking into account your hourly rate.

Figure 12.1: **MILESTONE WORKSHEET**

Project name: _____

Client: _____

Project completion deadline: _____

Milestone Description	Percentage of Project to Be Completed	Milestone Deadline (Time and Date)	Amount to Be Paid By Client upon Completion of Milestone	Notes

It's important to do research to determine what your competitors charge for similar services. When doing your research, find other freelancers or firms that have the same specialties, skills, and qualifications as you and who generally perform the same type of work. Be sure you understand what value-added services your competition offers to clients, so you can provide compatible or superior service.

Developing and Signing Contracts

A contract is a legal and binding agreement between two parties, you and your client. Before starting work on a project, it's essential that you create a written contract that both parties sign and date. As an online business operator, consider having a boilerplate contract that's easily downloadable by your clients, especially if the contract won't change based on the freelance work you'll be doing.

WARNING

This section provides basic guidance only and does not constitute legal advice from an attorney. Be sure to consult with your own lawyer before signing any contract or legal agreement.

Each contract should contain at least four key pieces of information that relate directly to the work you're being hired to complete as a freelancer:

1. A detailed description of the project you're being hired to complete, including everything the project entails. For example, if you're developing a website for a client, the contract might stipulate the number of individual web pages the website will include for the fee quoted. If you'll be doing custom graphic design work and creating a company logo for a client, for example, the contract should stipulate how many drafts of the logo you'll provide, along with how much time you'll dedicate to making revisions to those drafts before the client accepts one of your creations.

2. The deadline for the completion of the project, along with deadlines for reaching specific milestones leading up to project completion.

3. The price the client has agreed to pay you for your work. Listed here should be all additional fees and expenses the client may be responsible for. Be sure to list specifically when payment is due and how you'll be paid, as well as all other payment terms both parties have agreed to. For example, if a payment of 50 percent is due upon completion of half

---

CLICK TIP

If you can't afford an attorney to create and review your contracts, surf the web, download sample "work for hire" contracts, and use those samples as a template for creating your own. For Microsoft Word users, the Microsoft website (office.microsoft.com/en-us/templates/TC062562491033.aspx) offers a free "Work For Hire" contract template that can be downloaded and customized. More elaborate sample contracts can be downloaded from the following websites: aw-wrd smth.com/FAQ/work_for_hire.html, rocketlawyer.com/documents/legal-form-work +for+hire+agreement.aspx; urgentbusinessforms.com/contractor.asp; or webengr.com/services/website_design/terms/.

---

of the project, this should be spelled out within the contract, along with details about what constitutes half of the project. By the time you begin creating a contract, all price negotiations between you and your client should already be completed.

4. Details about who owns the work once it's completed. This includes ownership of or the right to use all related trademarks and copyrights.

Every contract, to be legally binding, must describe a specific offer and be accepted by the parties involved. Additional pieces of information that should be incorporated into your contracts include:

➡ The names and addresses of all parties (companies or individuals) involved in the agreement.

➡ If future work will be required, such as ongoing website maintenance or periodic updates, be sure to list information about how and when the work will be done, along with related fees. If as a freelancer you need to provide technical support related to your work, how much support will be included and how will it be offered?

➡ Describe how the final work will be delivered and in what format, if applicable.

➡ Depending on the situation, terms should be listed within the contract for remedying problems, such as disagreements and delays, as well as which party is liable for any problems.

- ➡ A cancelation clause in the contract should be included to describe how either party can withdraw or cancel the agreement and under what circumstances.
- ➡ Confidentiality clauses within a contract prevent both parties from disclosing secrets or proprietary information to other parties.
- ➡ Legal boilerplate clauses, such as a Limitation of Liability clause, should be included within all contracts. These clauses can help protect you from a legal standpoint and are something your lawyer will know how to incorporate into your contracts.

CLICK TIP

Ideally, a contract should be created or at least reviewed by an attorney, although it does not necessarily need to be many pages long and contain an abundance of legal jargon that's difficult for the layman to understand. What important is that the contract spells out specifically what both parties have agreed to in terms of the work you're being hired to complete.

Once the contract is completed, be sure to review it carefully before presenting it to your client. Then, don't begin work on a project until the client has signed and dated the contract and has agreed to all of the terms listed within it. Two copies of the contract should be signed so that each party can retain a copy for their records.

In business, problems and misunderstandings often arise. When one party fails to live up to the terms of what they've agreed to in a contract, this is referred to as a "breach of contract." Breach of contract is something you want to avoid because it can easily result in time consuming and costly lawsuits. By developing a comprehensive contract, both parties enter into the agreement with a full understanding of what's expected of the other party. This greatly reduces the potential for misunderstandings down the road.

Working with Clients without Meeting Face-to-Face

One of the biggest perks to having an online business as a website designer, graphic artist, or photographer is that virtually all of the required interaction between you and your clients can be done online. You can take on work from clients located anywhere on the planet and communicate with them via e-mail, telephone, U.S. mail, or fax, for example, and never actually have to meet face-to-face. For some freelancers, this is the ideal business model, especially if the work you'll be doing is virtually the same from client to client, such as customizing website templates; creating company logos, business cards, and company letterhead; or doing straightforward work on behalf of your clients.

Even if your business is 100 percent virtual (meaning no in-person or telephone communication), it's still possible and essential that you provide top-notch customer service. It also becomes more important than ever that your own website be highly professional, extremely easy to navigate, and effectively communicates your marketing/sales message. The website must then be able to transform a potential customer/client into a paying one and process the visitor's online order, all in a way that's efficient, quick, easy, and hassle-free for the people with whom you're doing business.

The one drawback to operating an entirely virtual business is that it is extremely easy for visitors to your site to click the "back" button on their browser if they get bored, frustrated, confused, and can't find exactly what they're looking for, or if you don't quickly capture their attention with your marketing message. You'll be facing a lot of online competition, regardless of the products and/or services you'll be offering, so within 5 to 15 seconds, you need to convince a visitor to become a client/customer using only the content of your site. Even for the most experienced web designer, accomplishing this goal is challenging.

Regardless of the products/services you're offering, all communication with your site's visitors must convey the highest level of professionalism. Your primary goal should be to offer the best customer service possible. Because your site's visitors won't be dealing directly with you in person or on the phone, for example, the content of your site should answer their questions, address their needs, alleviate their concerns, boost confidence in your business, and set you apart from your competition in terms of the quality of your work and level of professionalism.

Knowing who your customers are and understanding their needs, without direct communication with them, requires research on your part. Using the content and features of your website, you'll need to anticipate and address each visitor's wants, needs, and concerns, while at the same time offering a powerful and convincing sales pitch for whatever products/services you're offering online. In this situation, your online portfolio is an extremely powerful sales tool.

Avoid Unnecessary Confusion and Miscommunication

The easiest way to avoid confusion and misunderstandings with clients is to listen and communicate with them openly right from the start. Be sure to document everything and clearly outline the terms and conditions of your agreement in your contracts. Developing a clear understanding of your clients' expectations and then exceeding them in terms of the quality of your work will be beneficial.

Dealing Effectively with Client Problems

No matter how hard you work to avoid problems, there will always be difficult clients out there who will give you a hard time and never be totally happy with whatever work you do for them. The very best way to avoid client problems is to anticipate what problems or negative situations could occur as you work with each client and then in advance develop clear and efficient ways to deal with those situations without escalating the problem.

If a problem does arise, determine what it is and try to understand it from the client's point of view. Next, figure out the fastest, easiest, and most cost-effective way to properly and professionally address the situation and reach an amicable solution. Determine exactly what it will take to make the client happy, and assuming that it's possible to meet those expectations, do so (with a smile on your face). If, however, what the client is demanding is totally unrealistic or outrageous, it becomes your responsibility to negotiate a settlement so that the client remains happy with you and your work.

Being prepared to deal with problems by having solutions arranged in advance is one of the best ways of handling problems. Doing so allows you to act quickly and pursue a plan that's well thought out. Not being properly prepared could cause you to act emotionally or force you to act rashly and take steps that aren't in your best interest personally or professionally.

Even if your business is totally virtual, one of the fastest and easiest ways to solve a problem is to get on the phone or meet in person with the customer or client to properly assess and deal with the situation. Keep in mind that in order to make a client happy, it may be necessary to make exceptions to your company's posted policies or to amend the terms of your agreement. When this becomes necessary, keep an open mind, but be sure your own financial and legal interests remain protected.

Building Long-Term Relationships and Generating Repeat Business

Once you've developed a handful of happy customers, it's important to stay in touch with them in order to build upon the relationship and pursue additional work or repeat business. Periodic phone calls, e-mails, or regularly published newsletters are just a few of the ways you can stay in touch with past customers/clients and be available to them when additional need for your products or services arise.

Assuming your customers or clients enjoyed the experience working with you and your business, chances are they'll have no problem referring additional business to you or giving you very positive feedback. However, this might be something you need ask for. After completing a freelance project successfully, come right out and ask the client if he can refer you to anyone in order to pursue additional work.

Some freelancers offer incentives to customers or clients who give referrals that lead to more future business, perhaps a discount on future work or even a commission for the referral. Depending on the type of work you do and the relationships you develop with your clients/customers, tap your creativity to develop innovative ways to keep your past clients coming back for repeat business, and find ways those same people can help you find and land new business through positive referrals.

Of course, the quality of your work should speak for itself. Whenever possible, try to promote your own company name and/or website via the work you do for your clients. For example, if you've developed a website for a client, at the very bottom of the homepage, ask permission to add a link to your company that states, "website designed by: [Insert your name]." If you're a photographer whose work is being used in print or online, ask that your photo credit or copyright notice for your work include your website URL.

The trick to generating repeat business and positive word-of-mouth referrals from past clients/customers is to stay in contact with them and to provide an incentive for them to keep coming back to you, rather than your competition.

Growing Your Freelance and Online Business over Time

Hopefully, once your online business is fully established and you've developed a stable of clients/customers that is constantly expanding, the need to expand your business will develop. At the same time, as you figure out new products/services to offer, you'll discover innovative new ways to generate revenue using your website. The next chapter will offer advice about growing your business, hiring employees, outsourcing work, and developing additional revenue streams.

Chapter 13

Building Your Online Business

*T*here's a lot you need to know in order to be successful operating an online business and working as a freelancer professional who fully utilizes the web. This chapter focuses on additional information you'll need to handle the e-commerce aspects of your business and explores ways you can grow and expand your business after it becomes established.

Obviously, the online component of your business won't become mega-successful overnight. While you can establish an online presence relatively quickly (in a matter of days), it'll take time, money, dedication, and persistence on your part to make the online aspects of your business successful. Once your business is successful, however, refer back to Chapter 5 to discover additional ways you can generate revenues from your website by offering a greater variety of services to your clientele. At the same time, you can broaden your target audience and begin to tap an even larger potential market for whatever products and/or services you're selling.

It's important, however, to take one step at a time and to grow your business slowly so its operation and all of the tasks associated with managing your business and your clients/customers remain manageable. If you lose focus or spread yourself too thin in terms of how you spend your time and resources, you could hurt your business and mismanage your clients.

Fulfilling Your Orders for Physical Products

If you'll be operating an e-commerce website and selling products or downloadables, as soon as someone places an order from your website, they'll be expecting it to be fulfilled and shipped quickly, especially if they've opted to pay for rush shipping. To accommodate the demands of your customers, you'll need to establish order fulfillment procedures and a "shipping department" that maintains all of the inventory and shipping supplies needed to quickly get all new orders processed and shipped out promptly.

For each physical product (as opposed to a downloadable) you sell, you need to maintain an ample supply of appropriately sized boxes, padded envelopes, stuffing, packing tape, labels, and other shipping materials. Figure out exactly what you need and have a supply on-hand.

Depending on the shipping options you've decided to extend to your customers, you'll need to develop relationships with the United States Post Office, UPS, FedEx, and/or other shipping services in order to provide some or all of the following options:

➡ economy shipping—five to seven days
➡ 3-day shipping
➡ 2nd-day shipping
➡ overnight shipping

As an incentive to customers, some online business operators offer "free" economy (UPS/FedEx) or Priority Mail shipping (via the Post Office) by building these shipping costs into the price of the product. Otherwise, your website's shopping cart module will need to calculate shipping charges and add them to the customer's total.

If you opt to ship your products via Priority Mail or Overnight Mail from the U.S. Postal Service, free envelopes and boxes are available. Based on the size of your product, you may also qualify for a flat shipping rate. For details about postage rates and to order free shipping supplies from the USPS, visit usps.com. or your local post office branch.

To avoid daily trips to the local post office to buy stamps/postage and drop off your packages, you can arrange for a daily pick up with your mail carrier; however, each package will need to have the proper postage already affixed. Thus, you might opt to acquire or rent a postage meter from a company like Pitney Bowes (pitneybowes.com). Several models are available, based on the amount of shipping you'll be doing.

For a startup business that wants to generate postage stamps in-house in order to ship envelopes or packages, Endicia offers complete, low-cost postage solutions that allow any computer that's connected to the internet to purchase and print postage using any type of printer, including DYMO Label Printers (sold separately, starting under $200, dymostamps.com). Endicia postage solutions are available for PC or Mac computers. While the required software is free and can be downloaded from the company's website (endicia .com), there is a monthly fee of under $15.95 to maintain an account. You then pay the cost of whatever postage you actually purchase.

Depending on the shipping options you plan to offer to your customers, you'll probably need to open shipping accounts with FedEx, UPS, and perhaps other couriers as well. Opening accounts with these companies takes just minutes and can be done online by visiting their respective websites. You can also order free shipping supplies (envelopes, labels, and boxes) on each company's website. They will be delivered right to your door. When opening an account, you'll typically need a major credit card. To open an account with UPS or FedEx visit UPS (UPS.com) and FedEx (FedEx.com).

CLICK TIP

To quickly compare shipping rates among various couriers, visit iship.com/priceit/price.asp, redroller.com/shippingcenter/home, or http://pakmail.com/estimatorj.

The prices these companies charge to ship your packages are based on several criteria, including the quantity of packages you ship on an ongoing basis (volume discounts apply), the shipping services you use, the size and weight of each package, your geographic location, and the destination of each package. To save money, you'll definitely want to compare rates between these popular couriers. In many situations, quoted prices to ship an identical package will be vastly different. Also, you can save money by dropping off your packages at a FedEx or UPS location rather than scheduling a pick-up.

No matter what you're shipping, it's a good idea to use a service that requires the recipient to sign for the package upon receipt. This may cost you a bit extra in shipping charges, but it can eliminate confusion if a customer doesn't receive her order in a timely manner. Depending on what you're shipping, you may also need to purchase insurance for each package (at an additional cost) and/or use some of the other shipping services offered. Ultimately, you'll need to budget in all of these shipping-related charges, including the cost of items like packing tape, stuffing, and labels, and pass these costs along to your customer by building them into the price of each product you're selling.

As you pack each order and prepare it for shipping, make sure you use ample padding or stuffing to ensure your products arrive at their destination undamaged. When developing the shipping policies and procedures for your company, you also need to determine what will be included in the packaging with each order. Some of your options include:

- A printed invoice
- A customer feedback card
- A printed catalog
- A personalized "Thank You for Your Order" letter
- Printed directions for returning or exchanging the product
- Special money-saving offers for repeat customers

From a record-keeping standpoint as a business operator, you need to keep detailed records of your customers, and related shipping and order details. Depending on the e-commerce solution you choose, these tools may be provided for you. Otherwise, you'll need to acquire third-party software, such as ACT! (act.com), QuickBooks (insuit.com), or FileMaker (file-maker.com), to help you manage these important tasks.

It's essential that you be able to quickly track any orders you've shipped, so having the applicable customer and shipping information at your disposal will be important. You'll also need contingency plans in place to deal with a wide range of potential scenarios and problems, including:

➡ An order arrives to its destination damaged
➡ An order gets delayed being shipped out
➡ An order gets lost in transit
➡ The customer wishes to cancel or change her order before processing
➡ The customer wants to return the product(s)
➡ The customer wants to exchange her order
➡ The order was incorrectly fulfilled

Dealing with these and other issues, which will no doubt arise, will require you to interact directly with your customers as well as with the shipping company you utilized.

Remember, regardless of the situation, always strive to provide prompt, courteous, and highly professional customer service. Your goal should be to quickly transform any potentially negative situation into a positive one (from your customer's prospective) in order to retain her as a valued customer,

---

CLICK TIP

When it comes to developing your online "shipping department," even if it's a small table in your home and a cabinet chock-full of shipping supplies, the more automated you can make this process, the easier it will be to maintain accurate and timely records, and the more time you'll save doing paperwork.

---

generate repeat business, and increase your chances of benefitting from positive word-of-mouth advertising.

Managing Your Inventory

Depending on what you'll be selling, who you're buying from (wholesalers, distributors, importers, manufacturers, etc.) or where you're acquiring your manufacturing materials, one of the challenges of being an online business operator is ensuring you always have ample inventory on hand to fulfill your customer's demands. Being sold out of a product or having to delay fulfilling an order by more than a few days could easily result in an unhappy customer and a lost sale.

On the other hand, having too much inventory on hand requires an additional financial investment, warehousing space, and additional insurance. If you'll be maintaining any inventory in your home, office, or in an outside warehouse/storage facility, you'll need to acquire insurance to protect this investment. Your homeowner's insurance will probably not cover business-related inventory or equipment against theft, damage, or other mishaps.

Growing Your Business

Operating a freelance service and/or online business requires a detailed business plan to help you get started. Part of this plan should include a strategy for growing and expanding your business over time. Ask yourself, where you'd like your business to be in 3, 6, and 12 months, as well as in 1, 3, and 5 years. Then determine what it'll take to achieve those objectives and start implementing those efforts accordingly.

As your business grows and you generate more and more sales or freelance work, you may want to expand the functionality of your website, add new features, and/or start selling additional products/services. To generate repeat business, you'll also want to find creative ways to continuously update the content on your site, and give people reasons to return to your site often.

Transforming a startup freelance and/or online business into a profitable one takes considerable time and dedication. Once this happens, however, you'll want take steps to grow the business. Thus, you may also need to consider hiring employees or subcontractors, finding office space (instead of working from your home), and/or quitting your current job in order to operate your freelance and/or online business on a full-time basis.

To successfully transform a startup business into a profitable one also takes persistence and patience. Try to anticipate problems or obstacles you might run into and develop plans in advance for dealing with them quickly and efficiently. If you're prepared when you hit a snag, it'll take you less time and cost less money to recover, allowing you to focus your time and efforts on more productive endeavors. Being prepared and having contingency plans in place will also reduce your stress and ensure you're able to promptly and effectively deal with whatever situations arise.

Be sure to maintain realistic expectations for your business and its growth potential, stay on top of all of your responsibilities as a business operator (including those tasks you don't find enjoyable), and always stay up-to-date on the latest trends and technological developments in your field so you can address the ever-changing demands and needs of your customers.

Before the need arises, have a plan in place to quickly be able to hire subcontractors or additional employees to help you complete major jobs and/or handle a greater number of jobs or projects simultaneously. Determine, in advance, whom you'd like to hire, how much you'll pay them, what hours they're available to work, and what their areas of expertise are. Having a handful of specialists and freelancers on call when you need them will allow you to be totally prepared if you're hired to handle several large projects simultaneously, if you need to meet a tight deadline and don't have time to do the work yourself, or if you personally don't have all of the expertise needed to complete a job in a timely and cost-effective manner.

Use common sense when hiring freelancers or employees or when subcontracting work to other professionals. Remember, it's your name and reputation on the line with your client, so whomever you hire must adhere to the same

CLICK TIP

When you hire freelancers or subcontractors yourself, make sure you have a written contract in place with each person, so all parties know what's expected of them.

high quality and professional work standards as you, and be able to work well with your clients. Finding competent and talented people to work with might take time, which is why this is a task you should handle in advance, before you're stuck in a time crunch with one or more clients.

Finally, keep close tabs on your competition. Determine what they're doing and take steps to do it better—whether it's providing superior customer service, lower prices, higher quality product(s), more attractive customer incentives, a more professional looking website, or a more efficient shopping cart module. Try to learn from your competition's mistakes and at the same time try to benefit from their research, business practices and policies, as well as their overall business model.

There's an Exciting Future Ahead

The internet is growing quickly and how people use cyberspace to conduct business is expanding by the day. Now is the perfect time to establish your business online and to use this powerful tool to generate freelance work for yourself. The need for talented website designers, graphic artists, and photographers is growing. If you use the internet to promote yourself, conduct business, and interact with your customers, you'll definitely be able to expand your business and begin working with clients and customers around the world, not just in your immediate area.

As you've learned from this book, even if you have no programming skills whatsoever, it's still possible to design, publish, and manage a powerful website, online portfolio, or e-commerce site that allows you to conduct business and promote your products/services on the web. Be sure to take full advantage of the tools and resources at your disposal so you can reach as broad a portion of your target audience as possible and showcase your skills, talents, experience, and creativity in such a way that potential clients will literally line up to hire you and/or purchase whatever you're selling.

Chapter 14

Freelance Experts Speak Out

*F*or some people, adapting to life as a freelance website designer, graphic artist, or photographer after working for years for someone else is a welcome and easy transition. There will, however, be challenges you'll face, questions you'll need answered, difficult clients you need to deal with, and a bunch of new responsibilities you'll need to take on.

The goals of this book have been to help you make the transition to being a self-employed freelancer a smooth one, and also to demonstrate how the internet can be an extremely useful tool to promote you and your work, find and land new clients, and generate income on an ongoing basis using an e-commerce business model.

Once you've established yourself as an independent freelancer, adding the online component to your business model is a relatively fast and easy process. As you'll discover from this chapter, one of the ways freelancers can generate new business and find new clients is by bidding for jobs using a service such as Guru.com or eLance.com.

You're about to read three interviews with freelancing experts. Inder Guglani, is CEO of Guru.com, Dan Biegler is founder/CEO of DBdesign, and Michael Alahverdian is a freelance website designer who is pursuing two business models simultaneously. From these interviews, you'll receive valuable advice, tips, and strategies for becoming a successful freelancer Guglani and Alahverdian also discuss how to avoid some of the mistakes they made when they first become freelancers. But first, Guglani reveals how to find and land new clients quickly using a service like Guru.com.

Inder Guglani
CEO, Guru.com

Website: guru.com

For freelance website designers, graphic artists, and other artistic professionals, Guru.com is major resource for finding potential clients. When a company or individual is looking for a freelancer for a specific job or project, it posts a description of the job online and then accepts proposals and bids from freelancers who are qualified and interested in taking on the job.

To submit a proposal and bid, a freelancer must first register with Guru.com where a fee may apply. As jobs and projects are completed, clients post feedback about the freelancer's work on Guru.com, which helps the freelancer build up his or her reputation and land future work more easily. In addition to submitting specific proposals and bidding for each job they're interested in pursuing, freelancers are encouraged to post an online portfolio on the Guru.com site in order to showcase their work.

Using a service like Guru.com, it's possible for freelancers to generate business online with clients from anywhere in the world and then conduct business with those clients in a totally virtual environment, with no telephone or in-person contact.

How would you describe Guru.com?

Guglani: "Many people consider Guru.com to be like an online staffing or employment agency, like Monster.com, but our service has a very specific focus and is targeted just to freelancers. Our service does a lot more than just match up freelancers with contractors, however. For example, instead of posting a resume, like you would on a career-related website, on Guru.com, a freelancer is encouraged to publish a complete online portfolio of their work. We also offer all of the online-based tools that are needed for freelancers to interact with and conduct business with contractors. We are a complete transaction support platform.

"Anyone can go onto Google, for example, and track down a handful of website designers, graphic artists, or photographers they can potentially hire. However, a search engine does not provide any information about who these freelancers are or their skill level. Without visiting the freelancer's own website, you also have no way of seeing their work. It's then up to you, as the contractor, to track down and open a dialog with the freelancer on your own. Our service provides a complete online forum for learning all about freelancers and then provides the ability to communicate online so everyone's interests are met and protected.

"When a freelancer is hired to do a job, they typically want a down payment up front for their work. However, the contractor is not always comfortable giving money to an unproven freelancer they've never done business with or whom they've never met in person. Guru.com offers an escrow service, again, so both parties are protected financially. This service helps both parties overcome the trust issue. We also have tools for invoicing and billing, plus provide all of the functions needed for a freelancer to properly conduct business with a contractor, from the start of a project, until it's finished."

What types of freelance jobs are listed on Guru.com?

Guglani: "Every day, dozens, sometimes hundreds of new projects are listed and made available for freelancers to bid on. The most vibrant categories we have are for website design and programming jobs. Graphic design, writing, and illustration jobs are also popular categories."

What costs or fees are involved for a freelancer to participate on Guru.com?

Guglani: "We have a subscription model, but that's optional. If a freelancer wants to use Guru.com, but doesn't wish to pay the membership fee up front, then we charge a 10 percent commission based on their earnings from the service. If a freelancer earns $1,000 for completing a project, they'd pay Guru.com a $100 commission. If a freelancer pays the annual membership fee, then we only charge a 5 percent commission. Those who pay the membership fee tend to be the most serious about pursuing their freelance careers, and this becomes apparent when contractors are reviewing their proposals and bids, because it's made clear which freelancers are paying members and which aren't."

How does Guru.com differ from a service such as eLance.com, for example?

Guglani: "The differences have become blurred, because eLance.com has made a lot of changes and improvements to their service in recent years. What Guru.com offers is the largest pool of freelancers and contractors on the internet, which means we're able to post the largest number of new projects for freelancers to bid on. Our fee structure is also different from eLance.com. We have a lower cost of entry, plus lower ongoing commissions. We also offer much better support to our freelancers and contractors."

One problem with services like Guru.com or eLance.com is that contractors are looking to pay very little for the freelance jobs being offered. To land jobs, freelancers using these services are often forced to submit extremely low bids to do the work. How can a freelancer actually make money when so many people, who may or may not be qualified to do the work, are willing to do it for very little money?

Guglani: "eLance.com and Guru.com simply offer a platform for contractors and freelancers to communicate and conduct business. We do not set prices or establish the market value for work being done. What we have found, however, is that freelancers who have a proven track record and an abundance of positive feedback from past clients are able to charge more for their work. Contractors want projects completed cheaply, but they also want to work with highly qualified and experienced freelancers, and they're often willing to pay for that.

"What we recommend is that if you're first getting started as a freelancer, you submit very low bids for a handful of jobs in order to build up a track record on the service. We also suggest that you invest the time and effort to create the most appealing online portfolio possible to showcase your work. The contractors who use our site often rely on someone's portfolio and their past feedback to make hiring decisions.

"Guru.com allows freelancers to create an online portfolio that utilizes text, pictures, audio and video files. So, someone can post their resume, display their portfolio of work, plus post an introductory video of themselves, for example. We encourage our freelancers to post as much content as necessary to help differentiate themselves from their competition. For our contractors, we've made it easier to distinguish between the high-quality providers versus the low-quality providers who might not have the necessary skills to handle the available job or project."

For freelancers, what tips can you share on how to best use services such Guru.com or eLance.com to find and land new clients?

Guglani: "You'd be surprised how many freelancers don't invest the time or effort to create online portfolios that truly showcase their work. Not only should a freelancer showcase their best work, it must also be directly relevant to the types of projects they're bidding on. Only about 10 percent of the freelancers who use our service do a proper job creating their online profile and portfolio before they start bidding on projects. This is the main reason why freelancers wind up struggling to land jobs. Many freelancers are skilled and talented, but they don't take the time to present themselves well to prospective clients, so they wind up losing out on jobs.

"If you're a newcomer, your online portfolio is your biggest selling tool. It's also essential that you customize each proposal and bid you send to a prospective client or contractor. A huge percentage of freelancers simply submit prewritten, boilerplate proposals that have little or no relevance to the actual job. Contractors award freelance jobs to the person who demonstrates the best understanding of the project, who has the most suitable qualifications, and who provides a competitive bid for the project.

"Once you're established using a service like Guru.com, the feedback you have online from past clients becomes as important as your portfolio when it comes to impressing contractors. Freelancers with extensive feedback and a really good and relevant portfolio can charge more for their work and land the most lucrative projects."

In your opinion, what makes a good online portfolio?

Guglani: "There is no fixed formula for creating an online portfolio. It's important, however, that the portfolio showcase your core competency, talent, and skills in the most creative way possible. It's very important to highlight your core skills and specialties, so you can differentiate yourself from the competition and clearly showcase what makes you special. Don't just state what you can do in a proposal. Use your online portfolio to prove you have the skills and talent necessary to complete the project and provide the highest quality work possible. You'll be competing with dozens, maybe hundreds of other freelancers, all of whom say they can do the work asked for in a project listing. Only a small portion of those freelancers, however, are able to showcase work that demonstrates they have the experience and skills to do the work that's necessary.

"The missing link that does not appear in the portfolios, profiles, or proposals created by many freelancers when they solicit new work online using a service like Guru.com is that they don't properly showcase their area of expertise or what makes them unique."

How much work should people incorporate into their portfolio to avoid it becoming too overwhelming or confusing?

Guglani: "This, too, is a matter of personal preference, and there are no fixed rules. I recommend, however, that freelancers avoid causing information overload when someone looks at their portfolio. Marketing yourself online is very different from marketing yourself off-line. Online, you can't overwhelm the person looking at your portfolio. And, their attention span is very short. Within a few seconds, your portfolio and profile need to showcase why you and your work stand out.

"I recommend having some type of specialty or catering to a niche market. You may wind up targeting only 2 percent of the contractors looking to hire a freelancer, but to that 2 percent, you're special and will be in demand if you market yourself and your unique skill set and talent correctly. Being special gives you the pricing power and allows you to charge more for your work.

"There's one person on Guru.com who specialized only in creating animal illustrations. She charges at least $50 per hour and has to turn down work. There are, however, hundreds of other illustrators out there who charge less than $10 per hour and can't land any work. By developing a specialty and proving herself, this one illustrator has created a demand for her unique talents and specialty. Contractors who need animal illustrations are willing to pay top dollar for this artist's work.

"A freelancer must have it very clear in their own mind what their core competency is and then determine how to best market that to potential buyers, clients, or contractors."

In addition to having an awesome online portfolio, what else is required for a freelancer to be successful generating business online?

Guglani: "When a freelancer responds to a contractor on a service like Guru.com, they must provide a proposal and bid in order to be considered. It's extremely important that a freelancer's proposal be personalized and customized for each project. Very few freelancers personalize their proposal or speak to the needs of the buyer. The biggest complaint we hear from buyers is that out of all the proposals they receive, too few of them are personalized or address the actual project. Many buyers won't even read a proposal if it does not appear to be personalized and address their needs. As a freelancer, don't take short cuts and submit prewritten or boilerplate proposals."

When it comes to setting a bid for a project, what advice do you have for freelancers?

Guglani: "It's all about the perceived value you offer as well as overall supply and demand. It's important to figure out what you're actually worth in the marketplace and then bid accordingly. If you submit a bunch of proposals or bids, and they all get rejected, either it's your presentation that's bad or your bids are too high based on the current market value for what you're offering. Finding the right price point to charge for your work will take some experimentation and research. It's a trial-and-error process that has no easy shortcuts."

When a freelancer is reviewing all of the available projects online, how should they choose which ones to bid on?

Guglani: "First, find projects that require the skills and talents you possess and can readily demonstrate with samples of your work and your resume. Next, look for projects that are posted by buyers or contractors who have posted other projects in the past and have a good track record working with free-lancers. Just as freelancers earn feedback on Guru.com, buyers and contrac-tors also earn feedback from freelancers they've worked with.

"When choosing which projects to bid on, pay attention to the budget for the project that the buyer's description includes. If someone has a budget of $250 for a project you believe they should have to pay $500 for, don't submit a bid for $500, because that's not within the buyer's price range. Choose proj-ects with a budget that you believe is fair, and then bid and/or negotiate accordingly."

What other advice can you share about creating an online portfolio and profile when using a service such as Guru.com?

Guglani: "Before you start submitting proposals and bids, have a few people who understand your work evaluate your online portfolio and profile. Get a second and third opinion to ensure that your portfolio and profile truly showcase who you are, your skills and talents, and what makes you unique. Also, take advantage of all the tools available online so you can make the best possible first impression and overall presentation.

"Make sure your portfolio and profile focuses on your specialty and isn't too generic. The more specialized your skills and talents, in terms of reaching a niche market, the better off you'll be when it comes to differentiating your-self from your competition.

"Once you've landed a few projects, do whatever is necessary to complete the projects and provide the best work possible. Earning an abundance of positive feedback from clients is essential for your long-term success."

What is the biggest mistake you see freelancers constantly make?

Guglani: "The freelancer believes wholeheartedly that they're skilled and talented, and they probably are. However, they fail to showcase their talent and skills in their portfolio, and they don't properly market themselves with their online profile or resume. Knowing you're qualified and talented is one thing. Demonstrating it to a total stranger in an online environment (who you won't meet face to face) is another thing altogether, and this is one area where I've seen many freelancers fail.

"Another common problem is that a freelancer will have the core competencies to land jobs, but they then provide very poor customer service to their clients. Maintaining a professional and positive relationship with clients is essential, which means it's important to provide a high level of communication and top-quality customer service. How a client feels about you is as important as your technical skills.

"One other mistake I see freelancers make is that they value their work based on the number of hours they put into it. This is a mistake, because people with similar skills work at vastly different speeds. What might take you ten hours to complete could take someone else just three or four hours. Buyers are looking at the overall finished project and the value of the finished project to them, regardless of how many hours you've put into it. This can cause a big disconnect in the mind of the buyer. If you're not able or willing to complete a project for the amount of money you've pre-agreed to, regardless of how long it takes you to complete, don't take on the project.

"In the freelancing game, you need to provide a well-rounded package, which includes having the necessary skills and talent, the ability to market yourself, and the ability to offer superior customer service to your clients. You must also handle yourself in a highly professional manner from the start of a project to the end, regardless of whether you're working with a client in-person or through an online service, like Guru.com."

Dan Biegler
Founder/CEO, DBdesign
E-mail: dbdesignnj@comcast.net

Dan Biegler is a freelance graphic designer who conducts business as the founder and CEO of DBdesign. He uses an e-commerce business model to find, land, and do business with clients entirely on the web. He started his business four years ago after working for six years as creative director for a well-known advertising agency that represented very large companies.

After seeing a dip in the economy four years ago, Biegler decided he'd leave his position with the established agency and seek out other opportunities. Initially, he planned to take on freelance work simply to fill the gap in between jobs. However, his freelance graphic design business grew quickly and ultimately became a full-time gig. Like so many other freelancers who conduct much of their business by working with clients online, Biegler uses the Guru.com service.

You have become one of the most successful freelance graphic designers who uses the Guru.com service. What do you do differently from everyone else to be successful?

Biegler: "Early on, when I was establishing myself as a freelancer and bidding on projects, I purposely bid low in order to help ensure I'd land those projects. My initial goal was to complete a bunch of relatively quick and easy projects that I solicited through Guru.com in order to build up a lot of positive feedback from clients. After I developed a reputation and gathered feedback, I began slowly raising my prices.

"In terms of what I do differently, I focused initially on establishing a positive reputation as a freelancer. I use Guru.com to introduce me to new clients, but then I strive to generate repeat business from those clients, which is ultimately how I've built up my freelance business."

How important is generating positive feedback when using a service such as Guru.com or eLance.com to find and land clients?

Biegler: "Earning the best feedback possible is absolutely essential. Someone can have a top-notch portfolio that would land them jobs off-line, but when they're soliciting jobs online, what's just as important as the quality of your work is the feedback you've received from past clients. Often, it's a combination of your portfolio and your feedback that set you apart from your competition. I have found that potential clients put a lot of weight on feedback and testimonials when deciding whom they're going to hire, especially if the relationship between the freelancer and the client will be based entirely online.

"Positive feedback is critical to a freelancer's success if they plan to do business online. Clients are looking to hire someone who is a safe bet. Positive feedback demonstrates you're a safe bet in terms of your overall professionalism, which goes beyond just the quality of your work."

What types of services do you offer as a freelancer?

Biegler: "My specialty is graphic design for print media. This includes designing brochures, fliers, newspaper ads, posters, and anything else that will be printed. I have dabbled in website design, but that's not my specialty and not a service I actively market."

In terms of your online portfolio, do you have your own website?

Biegler: "No. This is a sales and marketing tool I know I need for myself and something I plan to launch in the not so distant future. Up until now, I've utilized an online-based portfolio I created as part of my Guru.com membership. If I were to give advice to a freelancer first starting out, however, I'd definitely recommend creating your own website to showcase your work. For me, I used Guru.com as my primary online marketing and sales tool. I tried out several different services and this one works the best for me."

After working for so many years at a graphic design firm, has starting a career as a freelancer lived up to your expectations?

Biegler: "I went into this with an open mind and didn't have any expectations. Initially, doing freelance work was just going to be a very temporary thing for me. I didn't expect it to take off the way it did. I was pleasantly surprised to discover I could earn a full-time living doing freelance work."

What would you say in the biggest challenge freelancers face?

Biegler: "The biggest challenge is definitely dealing with all of the competition. It can be a challenge finding clients who truly appreciate my talents and who are willing to pay for it.

"One benefit to working as a freelancer is that during difficult financial times or when the economy is slow, companies turn to freelancers because they're looking to save money. This opens up more opportunities, because from their standpoint, working with a freelancer is less expensive than hiring an established firm to do the same work. Companies want to receive the same quality of work as they'd get out of an agency, but they don't want to pay agency rates. Having the experience working as a creative director for an agency has definitely been an advantage."

What tips do you have for a freelancer looking to get started?

Biegler: "Start by creating the best portfolio possible. It should showcase your best work. I also recommend starting out by charging low prices until you're well established, and then slowly boost your prices as your online reputation improves. It took a while, but now, I am invited by companies to bid on their projects that are posted on Guru.com. Most of the time, I don't even have to find which projects to bid on, because the prospective clients come to me based on my feedback and portfolio.

"It's important to present yourself as professionally as possible. It's also important that you're extremely confident in your own abilities. The bids and proposals you submit must convey your confidence to the potential employer. You need to develop the mindset that you truly believe you should be awarded every project you bid on, based on the quality of your work, your talent, and your reputation."

What tips can you share about putting together a proposal for a potential client?

Biegler: "When you're soliciting business online and plan to interact with your clients exclusively in cyberspace, it's important that your proposal properly communicate who you are, what you're capable of, and describe in detail why you should be hired. Focus specifically on the client's needs and how you can address those needs. Figure out exactly what the potential client wants and needs, and then offer that at a competitive price. When people look at my portfolio, they get a really good idea of what I'm all about.

"For various types of projects that I tend to bid on, I have pre-created detailed proposals which I then customize for each job before I submit it."

Do you charge your clients a fee upfront or require a down payment before getting started on a project you're hired to do?

Biegler: "I don't. I charge my clients when a project is completed and when they're happy with the results. I personally have a price list for my work that I try to stick to within a 15 to 20 percent margin. I try to keep my bids in the low-to-mid range, based on what my competition bids. If the potential client posts a range for their budget, I usually try to bid somewhere in the mid-range of their budget. I don't try to be the lowest-priced or the highest-priced freelancer bidding for a job. I rely on my portfolio and feedback to sell my credentials, and then offer a very competitive and fair bid to do the work."

What tips can you offer in terms of creating an online portfolio that will get attention?

Biegler: "I personally believe that simple is better. I prefer to use only a few examples of my work online. I come from a philosophy that less is more. I also tried to keep the look of the portfolio very simple and basic, using solid colored backgrounds, for example. I believe that more than 10 to 15 examples in a portfolio is too much. Potential clients won't spend too much time looking at your portfolio, especially if it contains too many examples of your work, or the samples aren't directly relevant to the job they're considering you for. If I'm being hired to create a poster, my potential clients don't want to see a few dozen sample logos or samples of brochures that I've created. They only want to see sample posters. If you throw everything you have into your portfolio, you're spreading yourself too thin and taking away from what differentiates you."

Do you have any other advice for freelancers?

Biegler: "Only solicit and bid on jobs you know you can do and do really well. Stick to your area of expertise and focus on marketing yourself in that way.

Focus on marketing your strengths and taking on jobs that will allow you to utilize those strengths."

What are some of the biggest mistakes you see freelancers regularly make?

Biegler: "In terms of utilizing the web to generate business, I see first-time freelancers bidding too high for work they're soliciting through a service like Guru.com or eLance.com. If you're used to working for an agency and billing agency rates, you have to readjust your thinking and pricing model as a freelancer. Another mistake I see freelancers make is they give up too quickly if they don't start landing jobs right away. Persistence and faith in your abilities are important in this line of work."

Michael Alahverdian
Freelance Website Designer

Website: andrastos.com

Michael Alahverdian is a website designer for Wakefield, Rhode Island-based NetSense Internet Solutions (netsense.net). He has more than six years of experience, and extensive training in a variety of programming languages and website design tools.

Alahverdian currently works part time for NetSense Internet Solutions, and also works as a freelance website designer during his off-time. He is responsible for designing and programming dozens of successful e-commerce websites and knows what it takes for a website to achieve success in attracting and retaining visitors, and then converting them into paying customers.

Most recently, Alahverdian has created and launched the ThisIsTrue Love.com dating website, from which he generates ongoing revenue by displaying Google AdWords on the site.

How did you get started in web design?

Alahverdian: "I got started about six years ago, working for a small, dial-up internet service company doing tech support. When the dial-up business slowed down, the company started doing web design work, so that's when I started programming websites professionally. I work with **HTML** and ColdFusion mostly, but I am proficient with a variety of programming languages and websites design tools. ColdFusion is a server technology used for rapid application development.

"I do web application development for NetSense, but I also do web application development in my off-hours by picking up freelance projects. I have worked with many startup e-commerce businesses and have helped them grow over time. Once a site is programmed and fully operational, down the road, it will need to be maintained and updated on a pretty regular basis, so it's important to develop a long-term relationship with your clients."

What are the biggest benefits of being a freelancer?

Alahverdian: "For me, the biggest perk is being my own boss and being able to set my own schedule. I can also set all of my own personal, professional, and business goals. I like being able to express myself and my creativity through the projects I take on."

What would you say are some of the biggest challenges a freelancer faces?

Alahverdian: "Juggling multiple projects with different clients is a challenge. Clients often believe they're the most important and they don't respect the fact that you have other clients who have their own deadlines. The expectations of clients are always very high. It takes skill and superior time management skills to get everything done on time and keep everyone happy.

"As a freelancer, there will be times when you're very busy and have more work then you can handle, but there will also be times when things are very slow. From a personal finance standpoint, you have to budget for the slow times and be prepared for them, which takes proper planning."

How do you typically find your clients?

Alahverdian: "For me, I rely on word-of-mouth referrals. Periodically, I'll also search Craigslist.org and eLance.com for potential projects to bid on. Craigslist.org is a great resource for finding jobs and clients because it's totally free."

If someone will be doing freelance work virtually and not interacting directly with their clients, what advice can you offer?

Alahverdian: "In these situations, communication via e-mail is critical. Both parties always have to be on the same page in terms of what's required for the project and what the client's expectations are. As long as the specifications and deadlines for the project are clear, not having direct communication with a client should not be a problem."

How do you set your pricing as a freelancer?

Alahverdian: "I dissect each project and figure out what's involved and how long it will take me to complete it. I then add 50 percent to the timeframe that I calculate. Next, I do some basic math, based on my hourly rate and calculate a flat rate for the project. My bid will take into account my own financial needs, as well as the client's needs and budget. I typically offer a flat rate for a project, but that rate is based on my hourly rate, based on how long I think the project will take to complete and what will be involved."

What can a freelancer do to set themselves apart from the competition?

Alahverdian: "Build a great resume and online portfolio, and then do everything possible to obtain positive feedback and testimonials. Your goal should always be to obtain repeat business and referrals from clients, which is only possible if you keep your clients very happy.

"If you don't have enough professional work to showcase in a portfolio, consider volunteering your services to friends or charitable organizations. A great portfolio is what will land you jobs, especially if the people hiring you are not technical themselves. Once you have a great portfolio, keep your prices competitive."

How important is it for a freelancer to show off their education, degrees, certifications, and overall credentials?

Alahverdian: "Compared to being able to show off a really great portfolio, your educational background isn't important at all. What is essential is that you can show you have the skills, knowledge, and talent needed to complete a job you're being considered for. If you can do a great job at a competitive price, people won't care whether or not you've graduated from college and have a degree in website design, for example. In reality, some of the very best website designers are self-taught and have no formal college education. As a free-lancer, I have never been judged based on my education or lack of educational merits."

In terms of skills, what's most in demand for freelance website designers?

Alahverdian: "A really good grasp of HTML is essential. You can't just rely on Dreamweaver. You need to know how to program and develop a website from the ground up. Understanding how to build a dynamic website is also impor-tant. Because a lot of businesses will hire freelancers to maintain or update their already existing website, you need to have the knowledge and skills needed to be able to do this quickly and efficiently, using the latest website development tools.

"A lot of clients want Flash created. I've also found proficiency using PhotoShop and Adobe Illustrator is important. Another topic you should be familiar with is knowing all about website hosting options. You should be able to create a website and then be able to direct your clients in publishing that site and getting it online."

What advice do you have for freelancers about creating contracts with their clients?

Alahverdian: "Personally, I like to have everything set in stone with a client before we get started actually working on a project. This means creating and locking in a written contract that outlines everything, including how and when payments will be due. I typically require half of the payment upfront and half upon completion. Within the contract, I also stipulate exactly what's included.

"For example, when I'm creating a contract for a website design job, I will include within the contract a preliminary site map that will outline what pages I'll be developing and what those pages will include. I provide a sum-mary of the website the client is expecting, including a list of features the site will contain. The contract also lists all relevant deadlines."

When someone approaches you as a freelancer for a website development project, what information do you need to know to get started and how does the process work?

Alahverdian: "I generally ask them why they want a website. A lot of people have serious misconceptions about how websites work and what they're capable of. My first goal is to help the potential client develop realistic expectations and a good understanding of what launching a website entails.

"If you build a website, it's like placing a business card on the world's largest coffee table. Someone might stumble upon it by accident, but otherwise, nobody is going to know how to find your business card and call you. This is why marketing and advertising your website is essential in order to drive traffic to it. A website is something that needs to be properly promoted to a target audience, plus the content of the site must have a specific objective. For example, it can be a communications tool or an interactive brochure, or it can be a catalog through which you accept online orders. I help clients clearly define their objectives.

"After determining the website's purpose, it must be designed in such a way that it's attractive, professional looking, very easy to use, and comfortable for visitors."

What information or content does a client need to supply so you can start creating their website?

Alahverdian: "This will vary, depending on the goals of the website. At the very least, I will need all final and edited text that will be displayed anywhere on the website. Web designers are not the people you want writing copy. That's not our specialty. Our job is to create a highly functional and easy-to-use website. The client should also supply any other content, such as product photographs, video clips in digital form, audio, or other multimedia assets that they want incorporated into their website.

"The need for having professional-quality photos showcased throughout an e-commerce website is essential. Another key asset the client will need to supply is their company's logo. This will allow me to create a site's look based on the image and the color scheme of that logo.

"One thing I always suggest is that the business owner spend time surfing the web looking for websites that they like. If they can show me five to ten websites that appeal to them, based on look, design, and functionality, this gives me tremendous insight into what the client wants for their own site and it saves a lot of guesswork."

What do you think are the most important qualities a freelance website designer should possess?

Alahverdian: "First, focus on experience and credentials. Make sure you have experience creating the types of websites your clients are looking to have created. Second, develop a portfolio of work that represents your skills, creativity, and overall talent. Someone might have programming knowledge, for example, but not have the artistic or creative skills to create really appealing and professional-looking websites. Your portfolio needs to showcase everything you have to offer.

"I believe a website designer should have the ability to create sites from scratch and not just plug content into someone else's template. If someone claims to be an expert using DreamWeaver, they should be able to fully utilize the program to do more than customize someone else's work. A website designer should be proficient using HTML.

"It's also essential for a website designer be able to work with all of the latest versions of the most current development tools. Proficiency in FrontPage, for example, was impressive a few years ago, but this development tool is outdated."

Should a formal contract be created between the business operator and a website designer?

Alahverdian: "You should definitely create a written document that spells everything out and that's signed by both parties. The document should describe the work to be done and when it needs to be completed by. It should also state how updates and changes, or how fine-tuning to the site will be handled. This document does not have to be created by a lawyer, but it should be signed and dated by both parties and be considered a formal business agreement. The more detail that's in the contract, in regard to what's expected and what's desired, the better off you'll be."

Do you have any other advice for freelancers on how they can achieve success?

Alahverdian: "There are a lot of people out there who promote themselves as professional website designers, for example, but who don't have the skills or talent to handle this type of work. Make sure you have the skills and talent required to do this job right.

"Also, if you're a website designer, it's important to have a really amazing website of your own that prospective clients can visit. This is above and beyond the work showcased in your portfolio. Clients expect a website designer to have a spectacular website, so it's important that you live up to this expectation. Take the time that's required to create your own professional-looking website. It's your website and your online portfolio that people are going to judge."

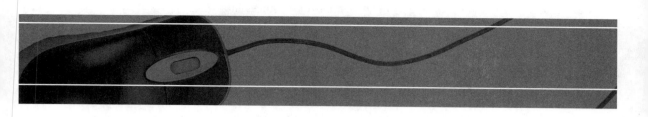

Glossary

*U*nderstanding the following terminology will help you better put all the pieces together as you brainstorm, design, and launch your freelance business and online presence.

Advertising. A paid form of communication that allows you to market and promote your products/services to customers by conveying your exact marketing message. As an advertiser, you have total control over your message as well as where and when it appears or is heard. As an online business operator, advertising can use many forms of media: newspapers, magazines, radio, television, billboards, and newsletters, as well as online venues.

Affiliate marketing. A marketing plan that involves getting noncompeting online merchants and websites that appeal to your target market to promote your online business by displaying ads or offering links to your site on their site. In exchange, you pay that site either on a per-view or per-click basis, or offer a commission on any sales that site helps you generate through a referral.

Brick-and-mortar retail store. Located in the real world (as opposed to in cyberspace), a traditional retail establishment you'd typically find along Main Street in your neighborhood or a local shopping center or mall. It can be operated by a local proprietor or be part of a nationwide retail chain.

Business plan. This is a detailed written document a business operator creates when developing an idea for a new business venture. Used to determine whether an idea is feasible, a business plan includes financial projections and forecasts, as well as a detailed description of the business' goals, strategies, operational procedures, policies, and potential.

Catalog page. The part of an e-commerce website that showcases the specific products being sold. A catalog page can display one or more products at a time and use text, photos, graphics, animation, audio, or other multimedia elements to help sell them.

Content. The combination of text, graphics, photographs, animations, audio, and other multimedia elements (also called *assets*) used to populate and create a website.

Conversion rate. This is the percentage of people who actually make a purchase from your website compared to the number of people who visit the site. As an online business operator, your goal is to create the highest conversion rate among your site's visitors as is possible.

Cost-per-click (CPC). How much it ultimately costs for each individual web surfer to click on an online ad for a website in order to visit that site. Some online ads are paid for based on the number of people who view them (impressions), while others are paid for based on the number of people who actually click on the ad.

Distributor. An authorized representative of a product manufacturer that sells large quantities of a specific product to retailers, who then sells them in much smaller quantities to consumers. As an online business operator, you'll typically buy your inventory directly from manufacturers, distributors, importers (if the product is coming from overseas), or wholesalers.

Domain name registrar. These are the online services such as GoDaddy.com and NetworkSolutions.com where people register their website's domain name.

Downloadable. A digital product such as a data file, website template, font, photograph, video file, audio file, or graphic image that can be purchased online and then immediately downloaded by the customer.

e-commerce turnkey solution. A complete set of website design and management tools that allows anyone to create, publish, and manage an e-commerce website for a predetermined (often recurring) fee. These solutions require absolutely no programming knowledge but a computer with access to the internet is required to use them because the majority of these tools are online.

e-commerce website. A website designed to sell products that will be shipped or uploaded to the customer once payment is received. Thus, this type of website must quickly and accurately convey details about the product(s) being sold and have a shopping cart feature that allows customers to safely and securely place their orders using a major credit card or another online payment method.

Experience. As you put all of your natural talents, skills, and knowledge together as a freelancer and begin successfully working with clients and customers, you'll develop real-world experience as well as a portfolio of work that you can showcase to future clients and customers.

Freelance professional (freelancer). Someone with specialized skills who is self-employed and seeks work from multiple clients.

Google checkout. A service of Google that is a way for e-commerce website operators to quickly and securely accept and process online payments.

Hit. A single hit is equivalent to one visitor to a website or one person viewing a specific web page.

Homepage. This is the main page of any website where web surfers land when they enter a website's URL into their browser software.

HTML. Stands for HyperText Markup Language. It's a popular programming language used to create web pages, online documents, and websites. HTML defines the structure and layout of a web page and allows for the use of hyperlinks.

Inventory. The quantity of a specific product you have on hand (in your warehouse, for example) to sell to your customers.

Knowledge. Refers to all the information you possess from your education and experience that allows you to meet the needs of your clients as a website designer, graphic artist, or photographer.

Logo. A graphic image that establishes a visual icon to represent a company. A logo can also make use of a specific or custom-designed font or typestyle.

Merchant. Someone who sells products or services. In terms of this book, it refers to someone selling products online using an e-commerce website.

Merchant account. Offered by a merchant account provider such as a bank or financial institution, this is required for a business operator to be able to accept credit card payments. The merchant is then charged various fees for the service.

Meta tag. This includes specific lines of HTML programming within your website that is used to categorize your site's content appropriately in the various search engines and web directories. In addition to the site's description, title, and a list of relevant keywords within the HTML programming of your site, you'll need to incorporate a text-based, one-line *description* of your site, which again uses keywords to describe your site's content. A meta tag must be placed within a specific area of your page's overall HTML programming.

Niche market. This is a narrowly defined group of people that make up a company's target market. The people in your niche (your target audience) can be defined by age, sex, income, occupation, height, weight, religion, geographic area, interests, and/or any number of other criteria.

Online portfolio. An online sample showcasing a website designer's, graphic artist's, or photographer's best work. It's used as a sales and marketing tool for landing new clients/customers and as a way to demonstrate skills, experience, creativity, and professionalism.

PayPal express checkout. A service of PayPal that is a way for e-commerce website operators to quickly and securely accept and process online payments.

Photoshop CS3 (CS4). An industry standard photo editing and graphic creation software tool used by photographers and graphic designers. The software is created by Adobe. For Mac users Aperture 2 from Apple has similar functionality.

Physical product. Any product that can be purchased online via an e-commerce website, but that needs to be shipped to the customer via the U.S. Postal Service or another courier.

Product. The specific item(s) an online business operator sells.

Public relations. A marketing strategy used to get free editorial coverage in the media in the form of product reviews, interviews, and/or product mentions in news stories, for example.

Retail price. This is the price that a merchant (retailer or online business operator) charges for a specific product.

Search engine. An online service that web surfers use to find what they're looking for on the web. A search engine is a comprehensive and ever growing listing or directory of websites and their content.

Search engine marketing. Also referred to as *keyword advertising*. It involves paid, keyword (text-based) advertising using Yahoo! Search Engine Marketing, Google AdWords, and/or Microsoft AdCenter. It helps to drive very targeted traffic to a site easily and inexpensively. These short, text-only

ads are keyword-based and appear when a potential customer enters a specific search phrase into a search engine.

Search engine optimization (SEO). This involves getting your site listed with
the major search engines and then working to constantly maintain and
improve a ranking/positioning with each search engine so the site is easy to
find and receives top placement.

Shopping cart. The module of an e-commerce website that serves as an interactive order form. It allows customers to input their order, shipping details,
and credit card/payment information in a secure manner, and then place
their order electronically through a website.

Skills. Acquired by completing a degree or certification program, by taking
individual classes, through reading books, by participating in online training programs, or through a variety of other methods. This knowledge is
used to perform work for clients that's related your area of expertise.

SSL encryption. Refers to the technology that allows safe and secure online
credit card transactions (payments) via the internet. Proper encryption
helps to prevent hackers from obtaining your customers' credit card data
and personal information. SSL stands for *secure sockets layer.*

Talent. Your ability to take the specialized knowledge and formal training you
acquire and put it into practical use in real world situations.

Target audience. This is the core group of people your business's products
most appeal to and who comprise your core customer base.

Traffic. Refers to the number of web surfers who visit your site on an hourly,
daily, weekly, monthly, or annual basis. A visitor is someone who surfs over
to your website to explore. Your goal as an online merchant is to transform
web surfers into customers who place orders for your product electronically when visiting your site.

Uniform resource locators (URL). This is a website address. A typical URL has
three main components. The first part typically begins with "www." or
"http://www." The second part of a URL is the unique name you must

select. The third part of a URL is its extension, which is typically ".com" but may be another such as .edu, .org, .net., gov, .info, .TV, .biz, .name, and .us.

Web browser. The software used by web surfers to surf the web. Microsoft Explorer, Safari, and FireFox are examples of popular web browsers. When creating an online business, it's essential that your website be compatible with all of the popular browsers.

Website template. A pre-created design that can be customized into a web page, website, or another piece of digital content. Templates can be purchased and downloaded online, and customized using web design or graphics software such as Adobe Dreamweaver) or licensed for use with a website or e-commerce turnkey solutions.

Wholesale price. This is the discounted price you, the merchant, pays to purchase products in quantity from a wholesaler or distributor. Once products are acquired for resale, you then mark up the price and sell them to your customers at each product's retail price. Your profit is calculated based on the difference between the wholesale price of a product and your business operating expenses versus the price you sell the product for.

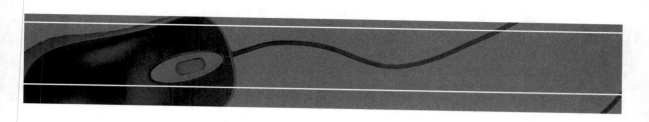

Index

Ad **Rich**

ess

The following books are now or will soon be available wherever books are sold and on the EntrepreneurPress.com website. For more information about these and other books written by bestselling author Jason R. Rich, visit his website at JasonRich.com.

Click Start: Design and Launch an Online E-Commerce Business in a Week

202 High-Paying Jobs You Can Land without a College Degree

Mac Migration: The Small Business Guide to Switching to the Mac

202 Things You Can Buy and Sell for Big Profits, 2nd Edition

Blogging for Fame & Fortune

Dirty Little Secrets II: Improving Your Credit Score and Managing Your Mortgage or Refinance

Entrepreneur Magazine's Personal Finance Pocket Guides

Buying or Leasing a Car: Without Being Taken for a Ride

Dirty Little Secrets: What The Credit Bureaus Won't Tell You

Get That Raise!

Mortgages & Refinancing: Get the Best Rates

Mutual Funds: A Quick Start Guide

Why Rent? Own Your Dream Home

Entrepreneur Magazine's Business Traveler Series

Entrepreneur Magazine's Business Traveler Guide to Chicago

Entrepreneur Magazine's Business Traveler Guide to Las Vegas

Entrepreneur Magazine's Business Traveler Guide to Los Angeles

Entrepreneur Magazine's Business Traveler Guide to New York City

Entrepreneur Magazine's Business Traveler Guide to Orlando

Entrepreneur Magazine's Business Traveler Guide to Washington, DC